THE EMPTY CHAIR

THE EMPTY CHAIR

The Teaching not the T-Shirt
with

Mike Boxhall

. . . a story that never ends. It is your life; take part in it . . .

The Empty Chair Teaching Foundation
West Sussex England

To my family, with love

Contents

Acknowledgements

Many people have been a great support to me in both my work in general, and my teaching in particular.

I always say that the groups of students are the real teachers but I cannot let this book go out without special mention of a few people:

United Kingdom. Several people have assisted me at one time or another; Henrietta Firth and Amanda Biggs on very many occasions and I am very grateful. Others have acted as sounding boards against whom I have tested concepts and received feedback, I think of my mentor and friend, James Low and also David Mostyn. In this regard I have to mention Andreas Bernsen who has endured more than 70 courses with me. Several enlightening conversations have resulted from this closeness. Mij Ferret, John Wilks and Vivienne Moss have also been there for me. Jo Féat has been a great help through many courses over the years.

United States. Coease Scott and Wendy Bridgewater were the first to sponsor a course for me, in Vermont. This led to a marvellous series of courses in Santa Fe, skilfully organised by Clare Bonser and in several repetitions in North Carolina and Florida, where I was assisted, organised and generally befriended by Pat Donohue and Sherry Phillips, to both of whom I owe a great deal and whose friendship I value dearly.

Spain. Carles Company and Toni Jimenez first lured me to Spain and I have enjoyed being in that country for several years now and teaching a large number of courses with their enthusiastic backing. Translation has been very important and Miguel Irribarren has done great work throughout. He is now also my book publisher in Spanish. Manu Mariño and José Aragües are regular course organisers now and a delight to work with. Diana Martinez is inexhaustible and has been responsible for taking me to completely new audiences. Throughout, I have been supported at so many levels by Carme Renalias, translator, and very good friend. I value her being.

Italy. Ida Ferrari with translator, Inke Richter, brought me first to Italy and we did several excellent courses together. More recently the planning has been sponsored by Hakusha, Brescia, under the direction of Silvio Mottarella and Laura di Lernia, the latter of whom has acted as interpreter. Recently a new star has been added to the interpreter team in the person of Chiara Garioni, who has also translated my book *Conversazione nella quiete* (*Conversations in Stillness*).

Ireland. My man in Dublin has always been the distinguished lawyer and mediator, Fergus Armstrong, who, like my minders in the USA, has often generously made me welcome in his home.

There are others, many others, including so many students who have contributed in a myriad of different ways. There are also those who I have specifically mentioned as my teachers in a separate list but throughout all, I am grateful to be married to Barbara.

Preface

This book arises partly out of my search for meaning in my own insecurity, a substantial goldmine of material, and partly out of interaction with many hundred students with whom, over the last fifteen years, I have shared and explored my insecurity alongside theirs.

After a number of years of this extraordinarily rewarding relationship, I found I was being continually approached to write a book. I found a deep and stubborn reluctance in myself to do this, as I experienced that the work, like the universe, is never stationary. Students proved to be equally stubborn, however, and eventually persuaded me with the line, 'You're 80 now, Mike, and not going to be with us for ever. Please leave us something we can hold onto.' I don't seem to have been very successful in teaching non-attachment!

I finally surrendered and promised to create a virtual book that I would add to in alternate months with no finite end in view. This is available at www.theemptychairteachingfoundation.com. In fact, so far, I have posted something each month. Because it is online, I also have the ability to change anything I have said at any time. Don't we all wish we could do this?

The whingeing did not cease, however. Now I have raised the white flag, and this book, *The Empty Chair*, is the result. I shall continue making the website postings for some time and, if they go on for long enough, there may one day be a second volume – like the first, created in essence by the students and the amazing synergy caused by their coming together.

About forty years ago, on the way out of a mid-life crisis, I started becoming a therapist. Training and then practising, first as a counsellor/psychotherapist, then as an acupuncturist, then as a craniosacral therapist, I was moving gradually into the body, discovering en route that the apparently surface levels of being contained the inner layers, and that whatever is innermost is not separate from the external form.

I found that the Cartesian mind/body split (as I understand Descartes' theory) stood up and was valid only from the point of view of an already split-off or disembodied intellect. I have experienced that truths of so many kinds are true in one context and then not necessarily true in another. This has been a big discovery for me and has probably made me a little more tolerant. 'If only I had known when I was 20 what I know now at 80!' is an expression of that thought.

After tentative toe-dipping in the ocean of experience called teaching, and quite happily advertising advanced courses in craniosacral therapy for practitioners, it gradually dawned on me (and probably first on my students) that I was not teaching techniques in anything. It had become a joint practice, and what was arising was an exploration of the embodiment of Spirit and the discovery that among the myriad expressions of the Spirit taking form was that which I choose to call 'Me'.

That first awareness that I have no inherent existence other than as a coming together of other concepts which, in themselves, have no inherent existence either is a powerful and, at first, unsettling experience.

Familiarity breeds contempt, people say, but perhaps more usefully it also breeds the awareness that in this particular truth lies the only security possible to us. If I am not separate from the universe, then I am the universe! Every time we turn that into a concept and wrestle with its awesomeness, we have lost it. Have lunch!

Slowly, again, it also became apparent that people needed no particular occupational label to be able to do this work – just the yearning to do it. A list of current students would embrace most occupations that you can think of. They include bankers, psychologists, teachers, housewives, lawyers, doctors, students, farmers, therapists, poets, dancers, physicists, philosophers, priests, oil producers, artists, tinkers, tailors, soldiers, sailors, rich men, poor men, beggarmen and, for all I know, thieves. But then, you see, I don't teach occupations. I walk the path with people, as best I can.

I am going to look at how these subjects have revealed themselves to me in my life, and ask you to walk the path of being more aware with me and see how it reflects in your own life.

It is my great hope that the work will lead towards some of us finding freedom from the disempowerment that unrecognised habits carry forward with them. Only when free of those chains can we be really useful.

Because no two paths can possibly be the same, there can be no didactic exercises, but there will be perhaps pointers at the moon. Please look at the moon, which is your experience, rather than at the pointing finger, which is the concept.

In 2008 my wife Barbara gave me a sturdy, rough-hewn wooden chair, made in a West Sussex forest, and the title of this book became obvious. The chair is pictured on the cover. It is an amazingly comfortable place of refuge.

The Empty Chair – The Teaching Not The T-Shirt

Foreword by James Low

The numinous is impossible to describe yet some flavour of it can be evoked so that it pervades our experience. This subtle work of making the elusive available is well accomplished in the following chapters. We are invited into the unfolding world of direct experience in a very relaxed, open and skilful way. Mike Boxhall expresses the richness of his sensitivity, as he shows through stories, verse, vignettes and exposition the way in which we can be invited into our own presence. Presence is the basic quality of being alive, the immediate vitality of awareness that supports and reveals all our experience. It is not a theory which can be grasped yet it pervades every aspect of our life. Perhaps this sounds mysterious yet as the author shows again and again it is through our ordinariness, our limits and our pre-occupations that we can find access to our ever-free presence. The path of being present here and now is found by not turning away from anything that occurs. We don't have to do anything new or unusual, simply attend to ourselves or the experience of our lives.

This may sound abstract yet as you enter these pages you will encounter the warmth of Mike's spirit, his facilitative enabling that eases our way into contact with ourselves. As far as I can tell this is not a book about anything. It seeks to establish no trust nor set out any dogma. There is nothing to be gained by it except more sense of your own presence, a presence that you already have.

Entering the practice of meditation and reading a book like this have some similarities. We have to open ourselves to what is in front of us, and then to simply be with it long enough so that we can receive what is there. Of course we have to be true to ourselves and read it in our own way as we experience being drawn more towards some parts than others. Yet perhaps our selections are primarily in the service of our beliefs and assumptions and so we affirm what we know rather than discovering something new. Observing how we make selections can help us discover something about ourselves as well as something about the book.

The generous and encouraging mood of this book is like a gentle massage for the spirit. Less striving, more ease, and as our striving and anxious pre-occupations fall away we'll be back where we always have been.

James Low

Introduction

The symbol of the empty chair implies that the teaching is perennial. It is always there. In each time and place someone will take the seat and voice the truth as clearly and honestly as she or he is able.

The teaching we are talking about is that expansion of awareness of Being that I call Spirituality.

Because the words will reflect the language and experience of the present, there will be resonance. Resonance is a spark; it aids ignition or re-ignition of awareness, and the potential expansion of awareness is infinite.

At several moments in history the spark has awoken an expansion of awareness that has taken different form in reflection of the time, place, space and society in which it ignited. We seem now to be in a period of mildly glowing embers in need of a fanning into flame. It appears most likely that the age of the collective is upon us and that the spark and awareness that it ignites must be a collaboration rather than a dictate. Another way to put that might be to describe it as *a joint practice* rather than as a new or resuscitated *dogma*.

Those thoughts encourage me to explore a pathway, from a purposefully personal point of view, in the knowledge that I do not feel any responsibility for other people's process, but trust that an exploration out loud by one ordinary person might help others to value their ordinariness and, indeed, relevance.

Much of what I read on the subject of Spirituality seems to encourage a negation of who we are and wishes to substitute another model from another time and place. It seems to propose that Spirituality can only arise in another language and culture. The market is full of such exotica and if we can afford it, we buy it. Such is the nature of materialism.

My right hand is held up in admission that the two seas in which I am immersed are Eastern and Western psychology as they have taken form from their Judeo-Christian and Buddhist roots. This is where I come from, in the former case by birth and in the latter case by conviction.

As you read this book, some parts may resonate quite profoundly, some may irritate, some may puzzle, some again may even make you angry. You don't agree, and that makes you angry. Think about that statement a minute: not agreeing *makes* you angry?

You could, if you wished, make this a real opportunity to expand your awareness by getting in touch with that feeling and where in the body it is located. By locating it, you have turned it into something that you can work with. It is a feeling; it does not represent who you are, but rather something that you can work with and let go of, if it is not useful. This immediately gives you the opportunity to be proactive, instead of being the puppet of your feelings. Instead of the feeling acting, you can act from the feeling. It is a hugely different statement.

Above all, be gentle. To notice that you have habits and to watch them at work allows the possibility of letting go of those habits. To beat yourself up for having a habit, to determine fiercely to get rid of it whatever it takes, is not useful. Being aggressive to the habit merely serves to inject a massive input of energy into that habit. Attention to it is raised, and this merely serves to give it nourishment and ensure its continuation. My hope is that the work will lead some of us towards freedom from unrecognised habits and therefore towards re-empowerment. We can be truly useful only when free of such chains.

Entering stillness

There is a great mystery about stillness, in the sense that it is not doing nothing and it is not a blankness – being spaced out – but rather the opposite. Stillness is a state of being very aware of precisely what is happening without being attached or caught up by it. It is more a state of witness.

Stillness is not something that we do. It is being – being at the centre of our true selves. This still centre is in all of us; we share that with the universe itself. This place in the stillness of the centre is dynamic.

> At the still point of the turning world . . .
> there the dance is.
>
> ('Burnt Norton'), T.S. Eliot

There is no suffering in stillness. There is an end to suffering in the reconnection with the centre. The function of healing, therefore, is to re-establish in stillness.

There may be times when we are surrendering to just being aware, rather than reacting to what is going on, when we notice that we have been lured into attachment to some thought or feeling – be it agony or ecstasy. At such a time we just notice *that* and become the witness of it rather than beating ourselves up for straying from the path. This tendency to beat ourselves up when we are not perfect is precisely the form of energy which keeps us trapped in reactivity and unsatisfactoriness.

Remaining in stillness

From time to time, once we have entered some conceptual path to wholeness, we actually experience the embodied sense of complete presence, stillness and freedom. We have not achieved this, in the sense of developing a skill. It is already inherent. We have merely got out of the way sufficiently to allow the revelation of what is actually the source of our Being.

Then something quite simple comes along and throws us off this razor's edge of balanced being, and we start grasping again and recommence running around the wheel like a hamster. It was always so.

This is the point of practice, this is the point of a community of people on sympathetic paths.

In the course of these writings, I repeat myself quite often, particularly when an important strong image seems to need re-enforcing. I do this in class as well and it is deliberate. Different people with different life streams resonate with different modes of expression. Hopefully there is at some moment an 'Aha!' of recognition and something has really clicked. I have learned a lot myself just hanging in there until the meaning is *really* clear. This is quite different from the nodding acceptance of a concept that everybody has heard before. Heard, yes, but not embodied!

Beyond stillness

While stillness remains a state that we fall in and out of, while stillness remains an object of my awareness, it is only the concept of stillness. The truth of stillness bears no thinking about. It either is or isn't and the essence of stillness is perhaps to be OK with either: to make it an object of desire is perhaps spiritual materialism. The object of materialism has changed from shoes to spirit; the subject has not changed.

The purpose of this writing will be to examine these concepts experientially; to see how we are disempowering ourselves by habituations that we keep bringing forward; to become more aware of what it is that we are attached to in the past and the future that stops us being present and, by becoming aware, to allow the possibility of change to awake.

There is nowhere to go, everything is in place, there is only the need to become awake.

The title, *The Empty Chair*, comes from a Buddhist concept. During his lifetime the Buddha asked his followers not to make images in his memory. For quite a number of years this wish was followed, but gradually, such is the all-too-human need to have an object of love rather than transforming oneself into Love itself (this, in fact, being the end purpose of his teachings), the chair or the pair of sandals or the symbol which were first used to mark his teachings were replaced by statues, with results that are now obvious everywhere.

Many Buddhists still recognise that the statues represent, as a mirror, the essential expression of evolved human life, but many others and certainly very many non-Buddhists see the statue itself as being an object of worship.

It seemed to me that the image of an empty chair represented very well the Buddha's teaching and that such an image could be the essence of all teaching on Spirituality. Daoists might rephrase this and say that what counts is the Teaching not the Teacher. The truth of this kind of teaching rests in its effects, the transformation that it may bring to the listener, rather than in the personality of the teacher.

As you explore the book, I am hoping it will become clear that the teaching is basically a group process, a revelation perhaps. I have often likened the work to making a winter stew. The taste and the nourishment to be got out of the stew will depend very largely on the nature and quality of what is put in. As trust in the energy of the group develops, so gradually even the more timid members are empowered to become fine cooks. The purpose of the groups is to explore Spirituality as an embodied experience, with the understanding that Spirit is not somewhere else or something to be achieved, but rather the essence of each of us right here and right now. To come into the full realisation of that, I may have to surrender some rather crystallised and obstinate views on the self and what that might consist of. 'Surrender' in this context is a good word, if properly used. The letting go has nothing to do with obeying orders: it is a result of realising habits that I hold and voluntarily relinquishing them.

The learning comes largely from the students' own life experiences. People hear their own and others' stories, sometimes in considerable awe. Often people hear and take on board their own life story for the first time in their lives. From hearing, they are able to heal themselves by fully acknowledging and then letting go the trauma they themselves are perpetuating and thus keeping themselves disempowered.

The teaching itself, as we have suggested, is perennial, taking appropriate form in different times, places and cultures.

The people

Groups consist typically of 16–20 people come together, mostly individually but sometimes as couples, from all over Europe, the Americas and sometimes further afield. People come to such a gathering for all sorts of reasons. I suspect there is a common core around a search for meaning, rather than simply gratification of want for something nebulously called 'improvement'. The common ground that I suggest is not always obvious and may take days, weeks or even years to rise to the surface where it can be articulated. Their backgrounds are various. In the early days they were largely therapists of particular models, but more recently there has been a deliberate effort not to be an exclusive and excluding grouping but rather to embrace anyone who is motivated. We try to avoid a 'better than' attitude to other people's work. There is no hierarchy of attainment – I hope! The very noticeable result of this attitude is that as no one is in competition with his or her peers, everyone shines. I have no doubt that if we have the idea that there is a way something or somebody should be, then lo and behold, that is the way they will be found to be. In any event, the how, the what and the why are all, in their fashions, limitations, so we try to work without them.

The work

The purpose of the groups is to explore Spirituality as an embodied experience, together with the revelation that Spirit is not somewhere else or something to be achieved, but rather the essence of each of us, right here and right now. To come into the realisation of that, I may have to surrender some rather crystallised and obstinate views on self. 'Surrender' in this context is a good word – the result of realising habits that I hold and voluntarily relinquishing them, not of obeying orders.

The method

A day's work goes something like this:

09.30–10.00 Meditation. Unguided and in silence. An explanation of the purposes and method of meditation is given if required.

10.00–11.30 Normally there will be a talk by the teacher (in this case, me) around any relevant subject that seems to resonate with what is going on in the group – an expansion of thoughts that may have been expressed recently. There may also be direct responses to questions that people have brought in.

11.30–12.00 Break. There are rather a lot of these. They provide space for digestion of stuff that is arising in people; they can also be an opportunity to eat chocolate biscuits and cake! Not unimportantly, the breaks facilitate a change of subject and a change of mood where that may be appropriate.

12.00–13.00 Hands-on connection, in pairs, normally one lying on a couch, the other in the stance of practitioner, either standing or sitting. Always fully clothed.

The form of touch is very light, the mildest contact, and the intention, fully explained in advance and re-explained from time to time, is simply to receive what is offered with no interpretation or reaction of any kind. The premise is that to be heard is to be healed, that few of us are ever properly heard, almost never without judgement and advice, and that this deep hearing is deeply healing. This is the theory and this is the experience of myself and others who have managed to surrender wholeheartedly the need to *do* something!

Some people will hold the head, others will be more comfortable at the feet, yet others may just gently place a hand on the chest and back. Actually it doesn't matter, if we have the attitude that to touch a part is to touch the whole. What I would rather people concentrate on is the stillness from which they approach the 'client', rather than wondering, 'How can I help this person?'

13.00–15.00 Lunch and walk or rest.

15.00–15.30 Meditation.

15.30–16.30 Verbal sharing of the experience of the session, from both parties. This is so important. It represents for many people the first time they have ever heard their own life experience being spoken out loud, or indeed have allowed themselves to connect with it at all. It can also be very moving.

16.30–17.00 Break.

17.00–19.00 Start the session and feedback cycle again, with the pairs swapping roles.

Times are only shown as a loose guide, as the reality is that the focus changes flexibly according to where it is needed in the moment. The overall structure is as set out, but the proportions of time allocated to this or that activity may vary.

At first, some people find the concentration required to stay present during the group sharing/feedback difficult; it is very easy to mentally accuse someone of 'going on a bit'. But as it gradually dawns that what is being heard is not only a unique person's life story but also the story of the human being, the human race, then a potent awareness develops – a recognition that this woman's story is also my story. I gradually come into ownership of an expanded view of who I really am, and that is never boring!

There is no need for the course facilitator to comment on these stories other than offering the occasional interpretation into a common vernacular. All that is required is that he or she should be a clean mirror. The power in this work lies not in the erudition of the teacher, but in the synergy of the group energy. Truly, the work does the work.

I like to talk of Intelligence at work, rather than the Intellect. This may not be very left-brained of me, but there does appear to be in all societies a mystical recognition that when the separateness of I/me is temporarily out of the way, then a communality, a field containing inner, outer and all points in between, which I call Intelligence, can be heard.

This voice, this revelation, can be trusted in a way no other experience can be, but trust means falling off the cliff, not conceptualising about letting go and hanging on to the bush at the edge.

In the book that follows, there are many examples of insights arising from the course of this work.

This book is not about Buddhism, at least certainly not Buddhism as a dogma, but rather it tries to follow (perhaps erratically at times) how Buddhism has expressed itself in the twenty-first century through the work of a group of people whose only point of communality is that they are people whose journeys have crossed around the particular fulcrum of their teacher.

The teacher is mortal, impermanent and more or less ego-bound. These two statements are not necessarily conflicting; it is possible for the teacher to get sufficiently out of the way, sufficiently unencumbered for the moment by his or her own ego, that the teaching can flow out unimpeded. Then the teacher and the students can all learn. It is truly a joint practice.

The work cannot be neatly packaged. Spirituality is not neat any more than the universe is. It is continually expressing itself in different form, as is the universe, and we have but to stay present to that, not organise it, as is the desire of the Intellect.

So the book will not have a neat sequential storyline. The chapters will tend to be reflections of what was actually there at a certain time and place, rather than the development of a dogmatic concept.

Gender is not a factor in this work, although the Masculine and Feminine principles, whether manifesting in man or woman, are important and these concepts will be discussed in a chapter on the subject. Generally, to avoid the clumsy composite pronoun his/her, I will rather arbitrarily sometimes use one and sometimes the other. On all occasions one should be taken to embrace the other. This seems a rather nice way of putting it.

We have discovered that transformation comes not from engaging insecurity in a war, which only serves to feed it the energy of attention, but rather from accepting it as a blessing that keeps us forever in the intimate and eternal present. Only in the present can we be truly proactive: to be anything other than in the present means to be reactive. To be constantly in the present is to be truly alive.

Whatever our lifespan, the one aspect of ourselves that is continually present is the body. I do not just mean the muscles and the bones and the organs of digestion and circulation; all sensory mechanisms by which we accomplish any thought, word or deed are part of what makes up the body. The body is not just a thing that tends to wear out and give us problems; it is also the awareness of that. The great message, surely, of Jesus and of the Buddha is that they were embodied – as are we!

The first half of my life was spent (probably the right word) in being a soldier and a businessman. That is not the direct concern of this book, other than to recognise that it is from such compost that the second half reveals itself. We tend to want to bury or throw away those parts of our life that no longer fit, but the parts we want do not exist without the parts we do not want. The secret is to *be* fully, not to be in denial.

This second phase of my life has fewer targets and I am content that it should reveal itself largely in response to the work that is going on through interaction with a widening group of students in many countries. Each student brings life experience and that experience is valued, even if and when it is uncomfortable, and from the acknowledgement of value comes the ability to digest and move on. The work, then, is about developing a form of practice that works, that at its best leads to transformation of insecurities into the gold that the alchemists sought, not the fool's gold of acquisition and greed that they were popularly thought to have sought.

Theoretically this work can be done on one's own and there are shining examples, throughout history, of lives that testify to that possibility. In an age like the present one, where all success seems to be measured in material accumulations of one kind or another, there are great pitfalls. We tend not to measure the effect of a teaching by how it touches lives, but rather more by how many students it gathers and how much money is raised. It seems more than ever essential to have three ingredients in place: first, a yearning to change; second, a teacher who is not dependent for his own fulfilment on his students' praise; and third, a group or community of other seekers, perhaps with nothing else in common other than the teaching, to share the journey. Without community, and speaking from my own experience, the ego is mighty clever at deluding us as to our progress.

'My teacher is better than your teacher; she is so much more profound. She teaches in 30 countries and has 40,000 students.' This and statements like it are not anything to do with Spirituality. They are expressions of what Chogyam Trungpa called Spiritual Materialism. The facts may be true. The work may be life-enhancing. The statement, however, is from the ego.

Throughout, I shall avoid technical or foreign terms as much as possible and will try to arrive at some sort of summary of the teachings, as experienced in this body, in the twenty-first century, at the age of 80-plus. Revelation of the Spirit, as experienced in the body, is the subject of the book. Let us walk the path together . . .

The expression of the work is as the body demonstrates it in the present time, in a Western cultural background. That does not make it better or worse; it just makes it real and present and available to anyone who accepts those parameters. It makes it possible for people of goodwill of other cultures to make interpretation from their own embodied and present experience. What we do not advocate is some sort of attempt to acquire Spirituality through dress and posture and speaking other languages. There is no advantage in collecting concepts unattached to embodied experience. There may actually be several disadvantages in collecting concepts at all, as they tend to be reified after a while and taken for the truth. In the chapters that follow, I attempt to avoid using technical terms of any nature. I have taken a view that if a concept cannot be expressed in the vernacular, then we are being invited to join an exclusive club and I wish to avoid that. I do understand that in some professions or modalities it is useful to have a special language that provides time-saving shortcuts. I suggest that this is not required in the expression of being more fully human.

I believe that if the reader gets some sort of mental picture of what is going on, what takes place in the retreats, from this introduction then the chapters that follow will have a better context.

All my experience tells me and constantly reinforces the awareness that working with the intelligence in and of the body accelerates exponentially the work that we do. What I love most about this work is seeing people change and transform through their own journeying, not through being told how they should be. The former is real empowerment; advice disempowers, however kindly offered.

We are not learning a therapy, but modifying and expanding our approach to life through the expansion of awareness of its source, right at the heart of who we are.

The teaching not the teacher

'The teaching not the teacher' is a concept that has been dear to me for a long time. These writings arise partly out of my search for meaning in my own insecurity, a substantial goldmine of material, and partly out of interaction with several thousands of students with whom, over the last fifteen years, I have shared and explored my insecurity alongside theirs.

Slowly, it became apparent that people needed no particular occupational label to be able to do this work, just the yearning to do it. A list of current students would embrace most occupations that you can think of, some apparently most unlikely. But then I don't teach occupations. I walk the path with people, as best I can.

We have discovered that transformation comes not from engaging insecurity in a war, which only serves to feed it the energy of attention, but rather from accepting it as a blessing that keeps us forever in the intimate and eternal present. Only in the present can we be truly proactive: to be anything other than in the present means to be reactive. To be constantly in the present is to be truly alive.

About twenty years ago I heard a saying of William Sutherland, a founder of osteopathy and a great visionary, certainly well before his time, who said, when discussing various rhythms in the body not associated with the medically accepted rhythms of heart and lungs but nevertheless palpable, 'You can rely upon the tide.' Once I had taken on board what I thought he meant by this seemingly innocuous statement, I was hooked and spent the next fifteen or so years studying just these six words and the implications of the existence of Intelligence, not subject to the Intellect. I continue, now with others, to work with these implications, not just within the field of bodywork of one kind or another, but extended to life as we live it.

These writings will expand on all the points touched on above and will explore how we can make the conclusions relevant. There will be some theory, there will be some reported practice and there will be, hopefully, a lot of work done. You are invited to join the work and to surrender, at least in part, some of the undigested data and reactivity with which we all identify, in return for a revealed truth. It is only true because it is embodied and does not remain just a concept of the Intellect.

What I, or anyone else, cannot do is tell you how you should be! I cannot possibly know that and a 'how to do' primer on Spirituality would be an impertinence. What I hope these conversations will do is serve as a mirror in which you may see resonance of your own expression of Being and, from reflecting on others' struggles to a greater level of freedom, find a way of letting go of some of the chains that you, we, all of us, carry. My own experience tells me that a degree of immersion in what comes up from within, rather than an analysis of the words, is what is required.

There is no success or failure, there are no silver cups or bonuses, there is only an expansion of awareness. The prize, perhaps the surprise, is to discover the clarity of who you really are, and this is beyond price. It certainly passes understanding.

Please join me in this exploration. I believe it to be worthwhile. I hope you will find it so.

I

Deeper Into Stillness

I do Nothing,
and the people transform themselves.
I love Stillness,

and the people bring themselves to correctness.
I do no Work,
and the people enrich themselves.
I have no desires,
and the people by themselves become Simple.

('The Dao of the Dao de Ching',
translated by Michael Lafargue)

A word that has been pivotal throughout this work is 'Stillness'. I first adopted Stillness in the 1980s as a thread that was to run throughout the teaching as a kind of keystone that held everything else in place. It is no accident, therefore, that the word 'Stillness' takes a prominent place in this book.

By placing the poem from the Dao de Ching at the head of this chapter, I am doing two things. One is to acknowledge the importance of Stillness as a concept and an experience in all my work, and the other is to pay respect to the Daoist philosophy which has, along with Zen, featured strongly in my own development.

I shall now expand on the sentiments expressed in the poem above and explore how we can make the phrase 'I do nothing' relevant to Spiritual growth. There will be some theory, there will be some feedback from practitioners and there will be, hopefully, a lot of work done by you and me together. I do think we have to put concepts into practice in order to make them the truth. You are invited to join the work and to surrender, at least in part, some of the undigested data and reactivity with which we all identify, in return for a revealed truth. It is only true because it is embodied and does not remain just a concept of the Intellect. I would dare state that if we were to engage in this work wholeheartedly, the world would be a better place. The perception is the only reality we have. The world is quite neutral; how we perceive it is the truth.

What this book will not do is tell you how you should be! I cannot possibly know that, so any attempt to impose such a structure would be impertinence. What I hope is that reading the book will serve as a mirror in which you may see resonance of your own expression of Being and, from reflecting on others' struggles for a greater level of freedom, find a way of letting go of some of the chains that you, we, all of us, carry. My own experience tells me that a degree of immersion in what comes up from within, rather than an analysis of the words, is what will be required.

I remember discussing with a group of 'old-timer' students in North Carolina whether we could condense the work down to series of headline words or phrases as reference points. We kicked this backwards and forwards for a while and came up with about a dozen. These, with a few additions, form the subject matter of this book. They will all surface, not necessarily in a linear sequence, but they will be touched on somewhere.

As my imperfect memory serves, the words were something like these: Stillness, Mindfulness, Presence, Trust, Surrender, Attachment, Ordinariness, Judgement, Being, Love, Emptiness, Insecurity. I am sure many people will think of others that I have left out. My experience is that whenever one immerses oneself really deeply in any of these words, it is possible to see many of the others at play.

On another occasion I tried the same experiment in England at our then newly opened teaching centre, Duncton Mill in West Sussex. The words and phrases were roughly the same, but there was an additional commentary. The story is this: some students had gathered resources together and presented the centre with a large, handsome Buddha statue. It weighs one ton. We set about preparing a suitable setting for this statue and created a large, circular, beautifully paved area in the form of a mandala, with a meditation walkway round the perimeter. The Buddha was lifted onto a specially made plinth and an 'eye-opening' ceremony was duly conducted by Ajahn Sucitto, abbot of Chithurst Monastery, which is nearby.

Going back to the construction stage, however, at the time when the group I am referring to was at Duncton Mill attending a course, someone wrote down the twelve words we had discussed and took the piece of paper, together with some flowers, and laid them in the exact centre of the site where the plinth for the Buddha statue was shortly to be constructed. A charming and devoted gesture.

The following morning, a fox – whose territory this was before we started clearing the site – was found to have left during the night his unmistakable mark of disapproval right in the middle of the piece of yellow paper. There are many levels of reality! The levels get realised when we are still, not when we are busy being reactive.

One of these twelve words, perhaps the most prominent in my particular view, is Stillness.

Stillness, as used here, is not just a lack of movement of the limbs or even a shut-down of the mind, but rather a state of Being. Stillness in this sense implies a 'not-being-caught-up-with' or non-attachment to whatever is manifesting.

It is perfectly possible that my brain could be buzzing and my legs could be twitching, but if I can be aware, peacefully aware, of those things happening and not identify with them, just rest as the observer, then I, the real I, am still. It is the brain and the legs that are moving.

> If water derives lucidity from stillness, how much more the faculties of the mind! The mind of the sage, being in repose, becomes the mirror of the universe, the speculum of all creation.
>
> (Chuang Tzu)

The important teaching in this quotation is not that the universe is still – it isn't, it is in constant motion – but that the mirror is clean and unobstructed. This means that my mind is in repose, aware of all movements, including the movements and excitement of my own senses, but just not caught up with them or attached to their activities. I cannot overemphasise the importance of this statement. So many people complain that their brain keeps chattering away when they are supposed to be meditating or being still. That is the nature of the brain. It does that. It is alive! The paradox is that if we can find a way of not feeding that activity with the energy of our attention, it may, like all forms of life when not nourished, just atrophy and give up. Suddenly there may come a moment when we realise that we have been in the space between the notes and there has been real stillness. What a beautiful music! The sound of silence can be heard!

This sound cannot be heard while we are busily trying harder to get rid of the chatter, but is already there: at the moment we surrender to the insecurity of not trying, not knowing, it reveals itself.

This is nicely illustrated by the following feedback from one student on her experience of being with another during recent training.

> I was feeling extremely tired and sitting with a cup of tea in the kitchen.
>
> Mary came and sat down with me and after a while said that she could see that I was exhausted. She took my hand in hers and held it on her lap and we continued talking about this and that.
>
> Then whilst general conversation was going on around us I could feel that she was giving me a treatment and it felt wonderful.
>
> I said to her, 'Mary – you're giving me a treatment,' and she just smiled. It felt like through her hands was a strength and a

> resource that was like a mountain. It was through the stillness that is familiar to me. I know this work, having been a student of Mike's and practising both as practitioner and patient.
>
> One thing that was particularly noticeable was when she then put her hand on my foot and seemed to be trying to make the treatment even better, the sensation of the stillness and the power of that stillness disappeared completely.
>
> I felt supported and enlivened by the treatment she gave me and it was really good to be in touch with that in her and in me.

This is exactly as given to me and emphasises the difference between the absolute receptivity contained in Being as opposed to the action of Doing. It is so hard to just Trust the Tide and be, isn't it? And yet, and yet, this is the only way we are going to transcend the limitations of our knowing and touch the core.

Here is an apposite quote from Erich Schiffmann from his book *Moving into Stillness*, (Pocket Books 1996), which seems to say the same thing in a different way

> Stillness is dynamic. It is unconflicted movement, life in harmony with itself, skill in action. It can be experienced whenever there is total, uninhibited, unconflicted participation in the moment you are in – when you are wholeheartedly present with whatever you are doing.

What a glorious therapy it is, then, to be able to sit in stillness with another human being or beings. Do we need the formal appellation 'therapy', or could we just cultivate this as a way of being? If hearing is healing, as we have often heard, then absolute stillness, non-attachment, provides the possibility for the story to be fully told and in the full hearing lies the full healing. We do not have to do anything, just receive, without judgement. There, in the receptivity, is the mighty power of the Feminine principle. How precious and rare this is!

Stillness is dynamic. It is a state of being where whatever arises into awareness is noticed, without the attachment that necessitates a reaction. We so easily react into doing something, whereas all that is needed is recognition, without mental commentary and judgement.

Stillness is not inactivity. It is, rather, the natural state of everything when it is not doing something. I think we could equate it with Intelligence itself which people call God, Brahma, The Dao, The Source, The Beloved and other names, before it takes form. There is emptiness of action but not emptiness of potency or awareness. The motor is idling; it is not in gear, but it is certainly running.

The value of stillness is that it represents the potential for the manifestation or coming into form of everything.

Where is stillness? Stillness is always at the heart of the present moment. Stillness is the place between the notes. Stillness is the place where I am not disempowered by all my yesterdays or my tomorrows. I am present!

If stillness is desirable, then we must consider what the route to it is. How do I get a piece of it?

This is the tricky thing about stillness. We can't achieve it; we can't acquire it; we do not earn it and we certainly cannot buy it. 'And again I say unto you, it is easier for a camel to go through the eye of a needle, than for a rich man to enter into the kingdom of God' (Matthew 19:24) means exactly that! We do not reach stillness by trying harder, but rather by surrendering our busyness, the incessant activity of the ego – the same activity by which the ego gets its sense of identity and precisely that which keeps it separate from its source. The rich man gains entry by surrender to God, as do all of us.

I would like to suppose that we have all experienced moments of stillness and have found those moments creative. Perhaps a moment when we feel completely at ease with where we are and who we are. There may or may not be someone else present, but there is no demand for any action or reaction. The situation just is and we receive it. If there is another present, be it a baby, say, or a lover, there is no demand; each receives the presence of the other and the relationship and herself in the relationship. This is stillness in joint practice. In all joint practice there is a synergy which is greater than the sum of its parts and this is the magnification of the power of stillness, of non-doing, inherent in relationship.

When I can cultivate this surrender and touch the stillness at my core, I experience that it is possible to approach another from that level of being and connect with him there. It is like saying we can approach the health of another person that lies under ('innermost to' is perhaps better) all their (and my) suffering. If we remember that at our core is stillness, then so it is at their core. The dramatic statement that arises from this is that to be in contact at that level of being is to be not separate, but one. There is no longer a me and a you. From this place of potential unformed comes the possibility of rebirth, right now. Such is the power of stillness.

People need to be heard. They do not need to be judged or told how they should be; they simply need to be heard in their pain, confusion and fear. To be heard is to be healed and to be heard deeply is to be healed deeply. I do not know where I first heard this, but I experience it to be true.

Being heard in stillness is like looking into a clean mirror: what is shown is what is. The mirror has no wise comments to make, no advice to give, it just reflects. If I can see what really is – simply, starkly, what is – I know what to do. In that moment I have become still, and in my stillness I have become present; and when I am present I am no longer the disempowered bundle of reactions that I am most of the time. I am at least temporarily awake. Awake, I can be proactive and useful; I have reincarnated from my disempowerment.

All this seems to be implied in the stanza at the beginning of this chapter. There is, too, a further point in the last line, that all of this is without intentionality, simple, normal, uncomplicated. It is the way that I live most of the time, in identification with my habits and patterns, which is pathological. Let us call it a state of suffering, or unsatisfactoriness.

The route, possibly the only route, to the innermost or core is via stillness, as any engagement or judgement will arrest the revelation. The intellect analyses. That is its function. But analysis, by definition, is a reduction to what can be understood and an arrest of flow.

Some years ago I spent a few hours beside Niagara Falls. While there, I wrote this:

> I spent quite some time beside these magnificent falls, studying the stillness in that incredible motion. There is something that moves and there is something that is just there and absolutely still. This I suggest, is the Spirit of the falls rather than its material. You can best appreciate this by becoming the fall.

It is said that the whole universe unfolded, and continues to unfold, out of absolute immanence. To be truly in the present where there is no past and no future could be said to be in touch with that immanence and the possibility of a different, unshackled, not disempowered way of being. The purpose of this work is the exploration of that possibility and one way to achieve it.

Let us continue opening to the experience of stillness as a felt sense in the body. If we experience it, good. If that is not what is being shown, good. Whatever comes into awareness just is and, by not attaching to it or fixing on it, a space opens up for something else to reveal itself until we finally get to the place that is within all form. I also call that place Peace.

I experience the grace of stillness in bursts. I wish, of course, that I could say I lived in it, but I recognise that this is my egoic self talking. I can think of two particular occasions when stillness took form and changed things for me: one was a couple of years ago when I was sitting in absolute peace in my garden one evening. There was nothing to do at that moment.

A sensation arose through my feet of a massive expansion of everything, incredibly powerful, very slow and majestic. There was also a sense of sound, although it was not audible. It was the Earth breathing and I was much moved. Was I mad? I don't know, but I fancy not, as throughout there was an awareness of watching myself having this experience and then trying to hang on to it.

The other was very recently, when on a break from working with a very lovely group of people, I stepped outside for a rest and just stood still. A very strange experience grew that the whole field of view and everything in it was pouring out of my eyes. That too went, just about the moment I started thinking about what was happening. Again, was it reality? I don't know, and does it matter? There are many realities.

At a much less dramatic level and more frequently, when I am teaching I become aware of some change of state. It is not dramatic and I recognise it as a parallel to the 'zone' that I have felt, many years ago, when I was an athlete. In this state, I trust what I am saying and just listen to it. There is no fear and all questions get an answer that satisfies.

Stillness is the source and what comes out of this source does not get filtered through the ego, so there is no fear in this state. I no longer have to worry about the status, experience or learning of the questioner. I just trust.

Then we all have a coffee and some cake.

I much enjoy e-mail conversations with Gil Siefer, a well-respected psychotherapist in New York and a spiritual adept whom I count as a friend and one of the Elders – a small, informal group of people that I have gathered around me as advisors on matters Spiritual. We are both of similar age and both suffer from the disease of continually asking, 'And . . . ?' I hope the conversations will continue. You may like to read a recent part of this conversation.

Gil wrote:

> I have come across some teaching of Ramana Marharshi about Stillness. I would like some feedback as to what he says Stillness is and I quote. 'What does Stillness mean? It means destroy yourself because every name and form is the cause of trouble. I am this, is the ego. The experience of I Am of being Still is the SELF.'
>
> Since your work is with Stillness can you accept what he is talking about?

I replied:

Dear Gil,

Thank you for that.

Ramana Maharshi was a great teacher. I believe that his internal clarity was entirely evident. His eyes expressed that clarity beautifully, even when his body was dying from a malignant and painful cancer.

That Self, that 'who he really was' – and is – was incarnated but was not the form of the incarnation, as best as I can possibly understand it from this unenlightened position. I think one could say that all forms, not excluding his body, are an expression of that Self, which was only conceptually and egoically, his.

I totally accept what he is talking about, in your quotation. Linguistically, I balk a little at the word destroy. I prefer the notion of becoming aware, in Stillness, a never-ending practice, of that which holds us detached from that Unity, and from that expanding awareness, seeing if we still need that separation, and if we do not, surrendering it. Effectively the same as destroying it, perhaps, but conceptually, less ego driven than destroying it.

I call the habituations that keep us separate from the Self, undigested life experience. They are an elaborate construct. Just that, something that we have painstakingly constructed in order to retain a self identity (this self, with a small 's' is, of course, the ego) resulting in a masking of that state of being that I understand as being Being itself, which we might also call the Self. It is a JOKE, that the source of all fear is a non-existent construct. Non-existent in the sense of not inherent and without substantiality other than in the relative sense.

I conjecture that absolute Stillness is not different from Emptiness, the potentiality of everything, not yet expressed in form. It is also inherent in the coming into form of all forms.

Talking about this, conceptualising this, is part of my attempt at becoming aware of all that stuff that I need to surrender. I realise that these words are not the experience.

I have no doubt that Ramana had the experience, solidly. I have just about experienced it in brief encounters and have then tried to hang on to it, when it has already gone. I think we probably all have.

It seems to me that there is a useful, relative Stillness, which is the observation of everything arising, call it chaos, without any judgement, just observation. The witness of creation, you could call it. I suppose the absolute awareness would be the experience of creation. If that experience were truly there, then there would be no difference between the creation and the creator. At the relative level there has to be a separate, pre-existing material from which the creation is created so, at the relative level, there can be no sense in the word infinite, it is merely a concept held by a self, which ridiculously, is somehow separate from the Self. NOTHING is not the Self!

Sometimes, I am very drawn to just sit, in silence. I think I might do more good like that. It does not appear to be my destiny, though.

Sometimes, I think the Self is absolutely, 'the Bliss of Being Ordinary'. Just getting on with doing whatever I am doing, in some sort of awareness. Wanting Wisdom is such a big distraction.

Sometimes, a zone shows up where I can just sit, quietly, or not, and listen to what comes out of the compost without trying to 'work' with it and I learn to trust that that is wisdom. The Teaching not the Teacher.

Much love,

Mike

2

A Spiritual Path

Spirituality, like the Dao, is a difficult subject to address. In both cases, anything you can say about it is really not worth saying as what is said will be words *about* something, not the experience itself, and will therefore be a concept. A concept is about a truth and is not, and never can be, the experience of Truth.

Stillness, Empty Chair, Teaching not the Teacher, Enlightenment and so on are all grand concepts and however long I go on and on, describing them, talking about them, reading about them, they remain concepts until they become experience. The implications of *that* are the whole drive of this work.

How, then, do we obtain the experience? Not, evidently, by thinking harder; nor, I suggest, by exercises, prostrations or repetitions of a mantra. These may well lead to a more disciplined and clearer mind and body, but they do not lead to the truth as experience.

And yet the Truth is there. It always has been and always will be. How could that not be so? Perhaps, as I suggest it, Spirit, Dao, Emptiness – Intelligence might be another word – are the very core of our being and what is required is not an acquisition but rather a surrender of that which keeps us out of touch. What keeps us out of touch is simply this: the separation from source which we know as personal intellect or ego; that fiercely defended construct called Me.

It is time we moved on from Descartes. Not to reject his enormous contribution to Western thought, but towards a more integrated Intelligence than the separated Intellect allows.

There is perhaps a form of spiral operating. First there was blind intelligence, then there was blinkered and limited Intellect, now there may be awakened *and* conscious Intelligence.

Some Buddhist thinkers talk about the Maitreya – the Buddha yet to come – as being a raising of collective awareness rather than a single enlightened being, whether male or female. This has certain resonances with the Christian picture of the next and last coming-into-form of the Christ. In either case, if consciousness raises *sufficiently*, then what need for further manifestations of form?

Another parallel between the two great traditions is in embodiment. Jesus was/is the incarnation into human form of God through the breath of the Spirit. The Buddha taught that the highest form of Being was contained in 'this fathom-long body'.

And yet, and yet, the dogmatic structures formed around the teachings of both teachers seem resolutely to repeat concepts and construct shibboleths, rather than listen to the revelation of those eternal truths as they express themselves in the body – the body that is always there, in so many different forms. We do not have to intellectualise or rationalise the form that Intelligence takes. We can, of course, but that will be to limit by definition or naming. The other way would be to just watch, in awe, the expression of the synergy of *all* forms responding to *the* Intelligence, without the limitations of Intellect.

This, as I see it, would be an expression of the Maitreya on the one hand and a completion of the Human Being on the other.

Perhaps this is what could lie behind the way we approach the subject of Spirit: as a revelation in the body and from the body.

I find it so satisfactory that there is nothing here, in any material sense, to be gained, or acquired. No one is going to control or monopolise something. The Truth is there only when we surrender separateness. It is sort of strange – or perfectly obvious – that the advances in technology, particularly in the field of communications, manage at the same time to make the Maitreya more possible and less likely!

What I am saying in a roundabout way is that there are many teachers out there on these subjects. There are some very good and honest spiritual teachers, some beautiful and honest books, and we could say, somewhat paradoxically, when we read about some of the more acquisitive behaviour of many people, that more words are being written on Spiritual subjects just now than at any other time.

Yet – and this is what I and some others are trying to address – where is the teacher or book that is equating Spirituality with the *revelations* of the physical body, rather than with intellectual conceptualisations *about* it? Many people work with the body in order to train it and the mind.

3
Awareness

Who I Really Am

No beginning, only Process.
The Spirit reincarnates.
Birth and Life
The meeting of the unfolding and the experience.
Layer upon layer of delusion.
I have become I and forgotten.
Yesterday was and tomorrow will be – or so it seems.
No now.
A tide there is,
An ocean then.
Beneath the waves,
There is only still.
The mother.
Pure awareness,
And I remember who I am.
The ocean stirs,
There is only process.

Mike Boxhall

The essence of what I am trying to say here is that work at a deep level, the level which we are calling the level of the Spirit, is an exercise in coming from a very deep place in our Being, not an exercise in refining what we do with greater and greater anatomical precision.

Most of the statements below will warrant chapters to themselves, but this is where I begin to lay out my stall and invite collaboration.

We do not do this level of work with the other – let us call him or her 'the client': it is quite simply the revealed outcome of the synergy created in the relationship that does the work.

Let me break this sentence down and explain what I mean.

Relationship, at this level, is what is there when that which keeps us separate – the personal intellect, the personal ego and perhaps the individual and personal soul – is surrendered. What is left is the communality of Being, that is Spirit.

Revelation is the arising (and falling) of forms, phenomena of whatever sort, out of the emptiness of presence, the eternal present, the now.

To let go of that which keeps us separate and approach the client from that place means that we touch the client at that level in her, whether or not that is held in her, or our, consciousness. A synergy arises.

When two elements approach each other in such a way that the scope of what they can achieve together far surpasses what they could achieve separately, they are acting with *synergy*. Synergy in this case takes the effectiveness of cooperation beyond normal expectations. (I owe this definition to *Chambers Dictionary*.)

The barrier to this level of work is that which I have described above in the explanation of relationship. It is very scary to surrender our sense of separateness; it is so well entrenched that we have come to believe that our life experience is who we think we actually are. In reality, that person, that image, which I have come to think of as Me, is nothing but a limited contraction of the arising and falling of essence into form.

The poem which heads this chapter tries to address the subject of such awareness. To be aware of who I really am involves me in an examination of the assumptions that are laid out in the first stanza. The second stanza talks of the descent into the unknown, the hidden depths of the unconscious, layer by layer. The final two lines treat of the revelation that the first arising from the Stillness at the utmost depth is awareness. Just awareness itself with no form yet, no separation between form and formless – process itself, without a form being processed.

Living wisdom

> How to make our lives an embodiment of wisdom and compassion is the greatest challenge spiritual seekers face. The truths we have come to understand need to find their visible expression in our lives. Our every thought, word, or action holds the possibility of being a living expression of clarity and love. It is not enough to be a possessor of wisdom. To believe ourselves to be custodians of truth is to become its opposite, is a direct path to becoming stale, self-righteous, or rigid. Ideas and memories do not hold liberating or healing power.
>
> There is no such state as enlightened retirement, where we can live on the bounty of past attainments. Wisdom is alive only as long as it is lived, understanding is liberating only as long as it is applied. A bulging portfolio of spiritual experiences matters little if it does not have the power to sustain us through the inevitable moments of grief, loss, and change. Knowledge and achievements matter little if we do not yet know how to touch the heart of another and be touched
>
> (Christina Feldman and Jack Kornfield, 'Stories of the Spirit, Stories of the Heart', from *Everyday Mind*, edited by Jean Smith, a *Tricycle* book) 1997 Riverhead Trade

Mindfulness

'Mindfulness' is a word that has been written about perhaps as much as any in the Buddhist literature. Perversely, therefore, I will limit myself for the moment to quoting a clear and simple explanation from a renowned teacher.

> The five spiritual faculties – faith, energy, mindfulness, concentration, and wisdom – are our greatest friends and allies on this journey of understanding. These qualities are most powerful when they are in balance. Faith needs to be balanced with wisdom, so that faith is not blind and wisdom is not shallow or hypocritical. When wisdom outstrips faith, we can develop a pattern where we know something, and even know it deeply from our experience, yet do not live it. Faith brings the quality of commitment to our understanding. Energy needs to be balanced with concentration; effort will bring lucidity, clarity, and energy to the mind, which concentration balances with calmness and depth. An unbalanced effort makes us restless and scattered, and too much concentration that is not energized comes close to torpor and sleep. Mindfulness is the factor that balances all these and is therefore always beneficial.
>
> (Joseph Goldstein, in 'Seeking the Heart of Wisdom', from *Everyday Mind*, edited by Jean Smith, a *Tricycle* book)

4
Attachment

Eternity
He who binds to himself a joy
Does the winged life destroy;
But he who kisses the joy as it flies
Lives in Eternity's sunrise.
(William Blake)

We are all attached.

Attachment takes many forms: we are attached to our nation, our lineage, our religion, our education, our choice of diet and particularly our illnesses. We are also, of course, attached to our families and a circle of miscellaneous loved ones, human and animal.

We are attached to life.

Most of all, we are attached to the notion that there is a separate entity, separate from all other entities, which is called Me.

Strangely, no amount of serious investigation produces that Me. I can find my foot and my liver and my thought and my emotion, but the being that owns these attributes cannot be separately located anywhere. A whole book could be written on this subject and, in fact, many have, but the upshot, if we allow ourselves to delve a little deeply – perhaps we would rather not? – is that what we thought was separate turns out to be an interaction between all forms arising from emptiness and none of them is intrinsically separate. We are a result of conditions, just that!

Nevertheless, we remain resolutely attached and it is my belief that instead of turning attachment into a dirty word and trying to get rid of it, we should do well to examine our attachments more fully, acknowledge them, give them a good airing. Only then shall we have a choice of being reactive or not to the attachments we have formed and letting them go or not. My take on this problem is something like this: I am attached to all sorts of things, I do not claim otherwise. If I try to get rid of my attachments, I am merely feeding the energy of attention into whatever I am trying to get rid of, with nourishing results to the perceived problem. The result is fairly obvious.

If, however, instead of being violent to myself, I can just compassionately bring the attachment into stark awareness and remove the judgement I hold about it, then a space arises in which the attachment can flower into something else. This is then a creative act.

For a therapist, this can particularly apply to the desire to make someone well. That is a massive hook and the effect of the hook is to ensure that the energetic relationship between me and the client is one of striving, not one of empty, relaxed hearing – the hearing that is, in itself, healing. This kind of intervention comes from my inevitably limited view of how the client should be. If only I can present a space big enough that the client fully expresses, not necessarily verbally, the entirety of his suffering, not just the presenting symptom, then an inherent enlightenment comes into play and Intelligence itself reveals, not just my mechanical best intention. The client may then hear, perhaps for the first time, a revelation of her true being which is none other than an expression, or coming into form, of emptiness. Sutherland's great statement, 'You can rely upon the tide', resonates with this.

Here is a little story from Carme Renalias in Spain which perfectly illustrates working *with* attachment, not trying to get rid of it.

> In one of the practices we did, I felt myself going into a deeper and deeper level, I could feel myself not being my body, not being my feelings, not being even myself on this time, just being like everywhere and time did not exist. And then, I don't know where it came from, the image of my children and all of a sudden

> I felt myself coming back and noticing I couldn't dis-attach from them, the fear of losing them appeared.
>
> I had been somewhere where I felt no attachment, no pleasure, no pain, just being, but the fear of losing my children was so strong that it caused me a lot of suffering, sadness to imagine letting go of my attachment to them. The sadness just was. It was important to experience it, because even though there was the suffering, I could see the path underneath suffering. From all being one, it became differentiation, my children and myself, love became fear. It still moves me now while I am writing it, it makes me feel very humble and very gentle with myself. In this life we become attached, to our family, our ideas, our teachers and as you said to our life . . . and we forget that all is one.

I think we must, as Blake proposes, cease binding ourselves to our attachment to 'good' and our aversion to 'bad', and just kiss them both as they pass. Thus we shall rest in the present and to be fully in the present is the sum of human development, fully expressed.

Please do not get attached to getting rid of attachment!

5
Ordinary

As I have explained before, I consider that the sharing we do, of the experiences that arise during the hands-on sessions, is probably the most important segment of the work. Important in the sense that what we are listening to is someone's embodied experience of the life story that they have identified with as being 'Me'.

If the group is safe and the trust is there, the revelation may well be at a deeper level than the speaker has ever allowed herself to experience at any time in her life. That is to say, she hears her story for the first time. The awakening to the disempowerments that we all keep on repeating can be very profound. The possibilities for choice that stem from the awareness can be equally profound. Once I come into the realisation of how I am habituated, the possibility of change is there. I have options which I do not have while I remain reactive.

Time after time, we have sat in a state of simple receiving while someone explores, sometimes in astonishment, how he has colluded in his own life-limiting disempowerment by accepting perceived parental judgements as being a statement of continuing truth about his value as a person.

Sometimes the change resulting from the empowerment of awareness is very rapid, sometimes the trauma has to be revisited and revisited, before the penny fully drops that 'Hey, I can do something about this. In fact, I had better, as no one else can!' Never mind *will*, no one else *can*.

It is almost impossible to exaggerate the privilege of witnessing these life stories. I have no difficulty in remaining completely present to them as I fully realise that what I am hearing is also the story of my life and the story of humanity. The imagery may vary from one culture to another, and from one generation to another, but the essence is perennial, changing only its form, not its essence.

Another thing we have discussed elsewhere and quite often refer to in seminars is the difference between the personal intellect and Intelligence. Briefly and very simplistically, for this purpose, the intellect relates to Intelligence in the way that a diode searches for and finds radio waves on a crystal. I am painting a pictorial analogy; I am not quoting a science. I have referred to Rupert Sheldrake and his hypothesis of Morphic Resonance with some gratitude when I get too depressed at the loneliness of not being 'scientific'.

Just recently, however, something new and, to me, enormously exciting has been happening. Instead of people experiencing anger or shame or amazement at the emerging revelations of patterns of reactivity and the awareness of 'how stupid I have been', they are beginning to talk about the 'ordinariness' of what they are experiencing, as they get in touch with deeper layers of the psyche held in and revealed through getting in touch with and acceptance of the body. It is not that there is no pain – there can be quite a lot of it. It is more that there is observation and sensation of the pain but less, or no, suffering from it. Can we separate one from the other? I believe so.

Assuming, as I have come to trust, that what happens in one group, in one place, tends to be already in place somehow, in the context of another group, in another place, and this is what I mean by Morphic Resonance, then there is a real breakthrough to non-attachment, or rather less attachment. When this happens, I feel that what I set out to do is largely done; we only have to guard against falling back into old patterns and lack of awareness.

I always claim that what I set out to do is *nothing*. My wife keeps reminding me that you can't do nothing – and I agree – but what you can do is *trust*. I am content with that correction.

Since beginning this work, some years ago now, the aim has always been to reveal what is actually there, when we go deeper into our beings, the human psyche, rather than take a philosophy or religion and try to match up to it.

By and large, I have tried to avoid dogma and '-isms'. I have largely avoided terms in Sanskrit, Chinese, Pali, Aramaic, Yiddish, Japanese, Persian and Arabic. If there is a truth, it has to be applicable in our age, place and language. We do not have to become someone else of another colour, language and time in order to be awake to our capacity. We have only to let go of the armoured defences, the separatenesses that create the diminution of the fulfilment of that capacity.

We try to hold a group as a safe place for all, by joint agreement and awareness. In that space, the sheets of armour are allowed to melt gently and we slowly become aware of what is left.

And what is left finally, turns out to be *ordinary*. The bliss of being ordinary!

There is nothing else. Just stay watchful and in communion, so that we remain aware of habits and how easily they can rush back into formation.

Throughout this work, the main reference points, to which I have to keep on returning, are the embodied life and example of Jesus and the life and teachings of the Buddha. I believe it to be valid to seek to be *present* with those examples. Where is present? Why, the one thing that is present from birth to death is the body. Even before the awareness of that fact.

> There is one thing that, when cultivated and regularly practised, leads to deep spiritual intention, to peace, to mindfulness and clear comprehension, to vision and knowledge, to a happy life here and now, and to the culmination of wisdom and awakening. And what is that one thing? It is mindfulness centred on the body.
>
> (Sattipathana Suta, The Buddha)

Ordinary enlightenment

The popular view is that in order to become enlightened we have to become something other than what we already are. Somehow what or how we are is inferior and gross. To become enlightened we have to get rid of all our imperfections and change ourselves through some sort of alchemical process into a kind of super-being.

The first and perhaps most interesting angle on this point of view is that it involves a judgement by someone who, in the same breath, is saying that he is not fit to judge! I am reminded of Groucho Marx who said, profoundly, that he would not stoop to join any club that would have him as a member.

The essence of Buddhism, in my understanding, is that we are already enlightened but have forgotten that. We have forgotten who we really are. We have come to think that we are the sum of our life experiences, ignoring the being that lies underneath those undigested residues that we have been unable to let go of and which bind us to the past.

Let's turn the thing around and look at it another way. If we are already enlightened, the task is to get in touch with who we really are. At least that is part of the task, because if we cannot trust our own judgement, we need to go further and come into the awareness of who we are, without judgement. Just gradually, or suddenly, take on board a greater awareness of who we are and how we are and accept that without wishing it weren't so, or were something else.

This, then, is the first level of enlightenment: awareness. Just that, awareness.

I am not saying there are no degrees of awareness of enlightenment. I am sure there are, but they are an expansion of this first step – a coming into awareness of who we really are, without judgement.

I have seen so many people strive to do their meditations and other practices, often for many years and very conscientiously, in the belief that out of the striving will come a changed person. Unfortunately, what comes out of the searching and struggling is searching and struggling! It seems so much more reasonable to me to believe that being born in a human body in this time and in this place is all the material we need and that what needs fully exploring is what being a human being means.

That means that if I feel angry, then anger is an attribute of being human. If I feel happy, fearful, sad, whatever, these are all attributes of being human. If I bash myself up for the one or praise myself for the other, this does not make sense as it is just a state I am in at the moment, not who I am. There is nothing blameworthy or praiseworthy in any of those emotions in themselves. If I can just note how it is without feeding the emotion with the energy of my attachment to it, it will go away as a new state of affairs comes in to replace it. Nothing is static unless we hold it so. Everything in the universe is in motion.

So, to go back to the subject of enlightenment. The main enemy to its revelation, remembrance, in all of us is judgement. By judgement I mean analysis and critical examination. This is what turns a revealed truth into a concept.,

If we are looking for enlightenment over there, that is not it. If we are seeking to find it through a programme of practices or austerities, that is not it. In fact, any path that puts enlightenment as something that has to be attained is not it. Enlightenment is not an object of the Intellect, but is nothing less (or more) than the absolute basic nature of who we are when we let drop the separation that is due to the suit of armour that we call 'Me'. There is no more duality.

I am reminded of Nasrudin. One evening, after dark, he was outside his house, under the streetlight, walking round and round, staring intently at the ground, apparently searching for something. Soon a crowd of friends and neighbours joined him, all wandering about under the streetlights looking.

After a while a friend asked him, 'Mullah, what are we looking for?'

Nasrudin replied, 'My house keys.'

Satisfied, the questioner and all the others went on circling and looking. After another period of this, by which time most of the village was there, someone either a bit more stupid or a bit cleverer than the others piped up, 'Mullah, where were these keys when you last saw them?'

'In the house,' said Nasrudin. 'But it is much lighter out here!'

It's like that. We look for enlightenment where the light is, where everyone else is looking, and all the time it is right here, inside.

6

The Bliss of Being Ordinary

Being ordinary is just so difficult! What we all want to be is special, separate, better than others, or, in some cases, worse than others if we insist on having an inferiority complex, instead of a superiority complex.

The trouble with being separate is that it puts us in a position of being very small and perhaps therefore defensive and reactive. In our separation we are just a tiny abstraction from what would be there if only we could realise our infinite reality.

We have talked quite a lot about stillness. Most of the time we talk about stillness as an object, a tool that we employ in our work. In fact, Dynamic Stillness is a state of being, not something we do, and could well be described as God looking out.

On one occasion someone described my work as teaching people to 'sit back and let fate do its work. This is a bit like watching someone drowning and saying they have the inherent wisdom to swim, so I will not throw them a lifeline. Yes, the inherent intelligence of the system knows best how to heal, but sometimes patients need help to access this and stillness and listening are not always enough.'

This, I'm afraid, shows an incomplete understanding of what stillness is. A lot of people talk about stillness and a lot of people include the word 'stillness' in their teaching. Very few of them actually seem to understand the state of being that is stillness.

If there were someone drowning, I would certainly throw them a lifeline. In fact, on two occasions in the past, I have gone into the water and got them out. In both cases I applied a pretty mechanical respiration technique. One recovered. The other did not. He had been under for 10 minutes before I discovered him and I spent 20 minutes doing mouth-to-mouth on a dead body before medics arrived and took over.

On the other hand, when people voluntarily come to me and say, 'There is nothing wrong, I just feel there is something else!' or, 'I seem to have lost something, somewhere down the line,' I just try to sit in absolute mental stillness and listen. In the emptiness the story gets told. There is no advice, no judgement, only emptiness. In the hearing lies the healing and the profundity of the emptiness reflects, very often, the depth of the healing.

You may be interested to know that the Chinese ideogram for 'to listen' contains five elements: ear, you, eyes, undivided attention, heart. Let us interpret this: 'I sit, with all my sensory mechanisms in gear, fully attentive to the story being told, listening from the heart, with no judgement.' That is to say, my personal process is not involved. I do not have to react. I do not have to give advice. I just have to listen. What a powerful dynamic this is! One, perhaps, that we cannot remember ever before experiencing.

Many practitioners from many countries come on courses quite simply to gain validation for their experiences arising from working with clients at very deep levels. These experiences are sometimes in apparent contradiction to experiences that they may have been taught they should be having.

Like almost every state or condition, stillness can be interpreted at many levels. It is worth repeating that there is a perfectly valid level of stillness which simply means not moving. There is another perfectly valid level of stillness which implies that there is movement, but that the watcher is not attached to the movement. There is a yet deeper level of stillness which is simply the source of all creation.

The difficulty always comes when one level gets confused with another. Render unto Caesar the things that are Caesar's, and to God the things that are God's.

This subject is becoming more and more important as far as I am concerned. It is crucial in all communication and relationships that the right level is touched.

The theme of *Men Are From Mars, Women Are From Venus* is the implication that if we don't speak the same language from the same place, we miss each other. We are not in touch.

To come from that place in oneself that may be described as Spiritual, it is necessary to surrender somewhat the demands and dictates of the Intellect. Perhaps we have to absorb the fact that although Intellect may be one of the myriad forms taken by Spirit, Spirit is not subject to the Intellect. By that I mean that trying harder, expending greater effort, is not the route to revelation of Spirit. The route is surrender of constructs, the greatest and the most complex of which is the personal ego. The ego is a construct and, it could be said, has no inherent existence other than that we ascribe to it.

I use the word 'Spirit' always in a sense that is communal, causal, a unity, not separate from all the forms it takes. I am not referring to something that is mine and differentiated. I acknowledge a personal Soul but am, in my perceived individuality, a form taken by the universal Spirit. By inference, I shall, when the time comes and the ego and the body have served their purpose, lose my sense of separateness.

It seems to me that the question 'What is Spirit?' is massively complicated, yet it is necessary to wrestle with it a little, or we shall continue to be judgemental concerning the relative value of ourselves and the works that we perform.

I believe and regret that I appear to cause confusion in some circles, as a certain number of people interpret what I say in class and in writings as suggesting that some sorts of work are in themselves better than others and that what I facilitate or teach is somehow better than what some others teach.

In fact, I have no such notion and people who have worked with me know and totally accept that. The experience that they have is of adding another dimension, or letting go of restricting preconceptions, with respect to whatever it is that they do, rather than finding an alternative to what they do. It's a case of and/and, rather than either/or.

This enhanced level of awareness emerges in the actions and perceptions of people performing quite mechanical tasks as well as people who have a more esoteric worldview.

This piece has so far, of necessity I suppose, been a left-brain conceptual explanation of the subject matter. Let me try to paint a few simple pictures.

I either take a piece of marble and I hammer and chisel it into the form of the Buddha, or I sink deeply into a meditative contemplation with the marble and just let the Spirit of the Buddha express itself. The need to chisel is not a retreat from Spirit, but rather the action itself is an expression of Spirit. There is, of course, an assumption in this example that I know how to be a sculptor, that I have learned my trade and that there is a skill available in me that facilitates the expression of that form and can read the marble. This is not likely to be an intellectual study, but rather a deep knowing. This was apparently Michelangelo's state when contemplating his *David*.

We can, however, extend from this sublime example and say that the Spirit may be equally present in such mundane actions as doing the weekly shop, washing up and cleaning the loo.

All actions, thought and speech can come from a mindful level and be done in full awareness, or they can be mechanical. I suggest that the difference always shows! In this context I am equating Spirit with mindfulness. There is a little pot of words – Mindfulness, Spirit, Presence – that interrelate with each other and sometimes we need all three to fully paint the picture.

The important thing is to get across the notion that while Spirit interpenetrates and is causal to everything, everything does not express Spirit.

Levels need to be congruent for there to be communication. That wisdom is seated in the heart, and is the embodied articulation of poets. That the heart is very clever in the way that it keeps firing and sending blood circulating round the body is a parallel but not spiritual statement. Both statements are valuable and coexist. One is not better than the other objectively. If you are a mystic or a doctor, the one may be better than the other subjectively – that is all.

Have you ever had a very profound experience? Perhaps an almost overwhelming experience that all things are in place and just how they should be? A 'eureka' moment, you could call it. And did you then try to share that moment by describing your feelings to someone else? And did you then, almost immediately, wish you hadn't? That is because you are talking at one level and being received at another. Just that; it happens often.

One of the great tasks of the approach to enlightenment could be to take the judgement out of awareness. This or that is. That's it. It is not better or worse. Objectively, it is. Whether it is better or worse to me depends on my undigested life experience.

Can any judgement be absolute? Can any judgement be objective? I doubt it. Because this is so, I believe we need to be immensely open and aware, when we approach the subject of Spirituality, that any and all of our strongly held views are mirrorings of our story rather than statements of Truth. Truth is there, of course it is. Where else would it go? But it reveals impeccably when the Truth speaks, rather than when we attempt to speak the truth.

Perhaps another way of putting this would be that when we are sufficiently still and not busy conceptualising, something very close to the truth will make itself known, perhaps through speech. The truth and the means of expressing the truth are one.

We keep coming back to the notion that it is the teaching not the teacher that counts. The corollary that has to be voiced is that we are talking about the truth at a particular level. All levels are valid at the level from which they are formed. It is not true to say that a truth at one level is valid at another level. Failing to recognise that has led to so much opinionated bigotry and violence.

At the deepest level, there can be no working *with* the Spirit in a subject/object relationship, merely a dynamic expression *of* Spirit.

This level is simply not attainable from the ego or the intellect. I have no doubt that the route towards a practice at this level is in surrender of that ego or intellect, not in bolstering the defences or weaponry – the flight or fight syndrome. One of the advantages of surrender is that when it is true, a felt sense rather than a concept, it becomes no longer necessary to say that someone else's experience is wrong. It is quite nice just to notice difference. Perhaps I am actually talking about getting older: it can be such a comfort not to have to struggle so much.

This is not a proposal to get rid of the ego and/or the intellect, but rather from time to time to surrender them to God, the Dao, the Spirit, whatever name you choose to give it. Surrender is not particularly popular as a concept. It has unfortunate overtones and is pretty scary. But here is a relevant quote: from the TAO TE CHING by Lao Tsu

> The sage never tries to store things up.
> The more he does for others, the more he has.
> The more he gives to others, the greater his abundance.
> The Tao of heaven is pointed but does no harm.
> The Tao of the sage is work without effort.

The strange thing about a spiritual path is that the deeper one gets into it, the more ordinary it seems – it is the ego that wants to be special – and what had been ordinary begins to feel horribly pathological, which in fact it is, as it never was anything other than a chronic accumulation of undigested life experiences.

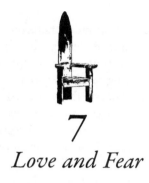

7
Love and Fear

> We have the habit of always looking outside ourselves, thinking we can get wisdom and compassion from another person or the Buddha or his teachings (Dharma) or our community (Sangha). But you are the Buddha, you are the Dharma, you are the Sangha.
>
> (Thich Nhat Hanh, from *Answers from the Heart*, Parallax Press) 2009

I think it would be useful to examine the words 'Love' and 'Fear'. I have been quite preoccupied with them both in recent times.

At the level of feeling or emotions they represent, in my thesis, the two prime emotional forms arising out of Emptiness. All other emotions are a step down from one or the other.

They are the great relative opposites in feeling. I say relative as, being forms, they have no inherent tangibility but are reactions, at the feeling level of being, to stimuli. 'When the conditions are this, that arises, and when the conditions are that, this arises.' There is a relationship or relativity between what is going on and our constructed sensory mechanisms. A joint practice, let us say. It is possible, in stillness, to watch this play.

They, the emotions, do not exist at any absolute level. This statement may, absolutely, be true; however, it is not useful to me at my relative, *Me* level, other than as a concept. It is only rarely an experience.

This piece that I am writing must therefore remain at the relative level, as must all explanations of concept. It is hard to get hold of, but all statements about the Absolute are conceptual.

In some of us, our feeling reactivity to situations, whether those stimuli be internal or external, is fairly well in awareness. For others of us, there is a dark mystery that can even overwhelm us to the point of our apparently drowning in an ocean of reactivity.

As with all opposites, when Fear is paramount, Love is less revealed and vice versa.

I perceive Love and Fear as being a unit, as it were, like Light and Dark; when one is more evident then the other is less so. When one is fully present the other is out of awareness. This last has been a very powerful thought. Nothing dies. These emotions remain part of the human experience.

There does not, I suggest, have to be an object. If we can cultivate Love, we are not getting rid of Fear, we cannot do that, but in proportion to our ability to cultivate Love, by bringing our awareness to it – to its revelation – we are diminishing our awareness, our attachment to Fear. Love, then, does not have to be projected onto someone or something, it is now the ground from which we manifest all feeling and the base from which we may teach. Whenever we come from the core or base, it is like being in what athletes might call the 'zone' . There is only what is without any particular, obvious, separate cause. We can let the work do the work, the body perform its very best, or, in the case of teaching, just listen to the teaching that comes out. Perhaps one can say the teaching speaks and I just hear what is coming out. There is, in that moment, however long it lasts, no 'me' that needs to construct something. (It has, in this moment, occurred to me that the same paradigm operates everywhere, in all aspects of our life, not just in the field of feelings – but perhaps that is another story.)

I have come to say that we manifest feeling, rather than feeling manifests in us, as I believe the forms that feelings take are a reflection or expression of our undigested life experience, rather than something given. We are victims in the sense that we are not aware of that, but allow ourselves to be largely reactive to a stored and unreleased collection of emotional experiences which are no longer happening.

Is this definition of suffering – because that is what it really is – difficult from the Christian viewpoint? (The Christian viewpoint is multifaceted, as is the Buddhist viewpoint. They are both many levelled and I extend this suggestion to all religions.) I am not sure that it needs to be difficult. 'Do you not *know* that your body is the temple of the indwelling Holy Spirit?' (1 Corinthians 6; I have italicised *know* to resonate with 'to be aware'). St Teresa of Avila states quite firmly that the prime study needs to be of ourselves.

In the same way that I suggested that Love and Fear do not have to be projected but known in their essence, so I further suggest that gnosis does not have to be projected but reveals itself from the Holy Spirit which is indwelling.

I have often used the word 'revelation'. Revelation does not occur in busyness. In busyness, space is too crowded with experience for there to be room for expansion of awareness.

Emptiness is rare, but a cultivation of non-attachment to what arises in the play of mind serves well to keep undernourished the dance of form, energised as it is by attention. Stillness is not a doing, it is a state of inattention to the dance. We should be better served, perhaps, if we were to combine fuller awareness of our emotions (they need to be heard) with less feeding of them through trying to get rid of them in the analytic reification of some psychotherapeutic models.

'And the peace of God, which passeth all understanding, shall keep your hearts and minds through Christ Jesus' (Philippians 4:7). What does 'passing all understanding' mean if not outside, not subject to, the intellect?

Perhaps this quote resonates with the statement 'Nirvana is beyond extremes', one of the Four Seals, as they are called, which define a Buddhist. 'Beyond extremes' means, in this case, not subject to definition by the intellect, or 'passing all understanding'. 'If we penetrate the nature of reality, it is also possible to achieve that cessation within our minds and as the fourth seal states, such a cessation or liberation is true peace' (The Dalai Lama).

I submit that the Christian and the Buddhist standpoints are so similar in that revelation arises out of Spirit/Emptiness, in both cases indefinable, and takes form in the relative Me. The relative Me is that in which God lives but is not God. Other than at the Absolute level, which I cannot comprehend, or I should have reduced the Absolute to a concept, an object!

You are all Buddhas! Wake to that!

I would much rather rest in peace than bliss, which is reactive. Peace, you could say, is proactive. I like that concept very much.

Somehow, this small offering came out of a quote by Jacob Needleman, of Anthony Bloom (Metropolitan Anthony), reported in *Lost Christianity*. Jeremy P. Tarcher/Penguin 1980, Anthony says, 'In prayer one is vulnerable, not enthusiastic. And then these rituals have such force. They hit you like a locomotive. You must be not enthusiastic or rejecting – but only open. This is the whole aim of asceticism; to become open.' I read this and thought of the saying, 'let the work do the work', and realised once again that we are all actually one, the rest is dogma . . . and wept for joy.

Is Peace, then, the peace that passeth all understanding, the substrate of both Love and Fear? I experience that it is, but I do not know how to turn it on!

It *is*. Just that, when all else is surrendered and the struggling to *understand* is relinquished.

The ideas in this chapter are beautifully illustrated in some feedback I recently received from Nicola Davies.

> Wow, Mike. That has just about summed up my week in France last week. The strong resistance to going there, the bewilderment and utter confusion I have felt for months now. I felt like a caged animal a lot of the time last week, restless but very energised (I only slept 2 or 3 hours max each night) and also there

was a deep sense of mistrust towards my captors. I often looked to the hill behind where you sit and had such a longing to run up the hill into the woods at the top – I felt wild, full of mischief and playfulness and there was a deep longing to be free. It was extremely difficult for me to come to France. The resistance was enormous but something got me there. A week before the course I had been walking in the woods with my dogs and I had suddenly stopped with a thunderbolt realisation that there was nothing I could do anymore, I simply had to let go and that was that – it wasn't up for negotiation. That was what I did every morning in the boat at the Mill, I just asked for help to give me the courage to be with whatever came up and to stop running from it. On the Thursday something shifted and I guess sunk to a new level or became embodied. A little more trust came, the possibility that it is OK to be here (I mean be alive here) and a huge sense of relief. After Embodiment 2 I felt so angry with you, Mike (for 3 months in fact) and I was disillusioned with you and the work and that was very uncomfortable. I don't know what got me to France but something knew I had to go and I'm very pleased I did. My heart has been hurting so much the last few months and I told you I had been having palpitations and it had felt like I had a vice crushing my chest – it had prevented me from running, something I have always done. This morning I went for a long run, but it was different, my chest felt free and also I felt I wasn't running out of anger, I was running for the joy of running, because I could, because I was free to do so – and it felt wonderful. As usual I can't find the words.

Thank you, Mike. With lots of love from Nicola.

All of us in the group felt much moved by the shining serenity of Nicola on the last day. The work had done the work and we had all been blessed. Michael, one of our number, voiced it as follows: 'I think the most satisfying aspect of the three-part course was the radiant peace emanating from Nicola at the end of the week.'

For someone
At the journey's end,
Freed of sorrow
Liberated in all ways,
Released from all bonds,
No fever exists.
(*The Dhammapada*)

As I begin to relate to it, the journey is into awareness, in the present, not a linear progress through this conceptual life. The sorrow is attachment to the insubstantial. Freedom is in presence, not reactivity, the bonds are undigested life experience and the fever is intellectual striving.

8

The Blessing of Insecurity

Following on from Fear, discussed in the last chapter, we should now look at Insecurity, a step down from Fear. Most of my work has been constructed around how to work with Insecurity, of which I have plenty, and turning it into an asset.

> If, according to Erich Fromm, the emergence of the 'mature man' is the aim of both Oriental Zen and Occidental psychoanalysis, and if the man on that level has shed his petty fears of insecurity, his one-sided logically reasoned propensity, there is hope for human beings to arrive at a better grasp of the meaning of reality. That this implies the shedding of greed in all forms and the overcoming of ego-worship goes without saying. Thus satori or what we attempt to define as enlightenment may, in the final analysis, be instrumental in a person's emergence on the apex of maturity in its widest possible connotation and within a thoroughly humanistic frame of reference.
>
> (Paul Neumarkt) in *Journal of Evolutionary Psychology* 2002

It is important to note that Fromm is quoted as saying 'shed his petty fears of insecurity'. He does not say, 'shed his Insecurity'. Being, I suppose, highly insecure, I take great comfort from that statement.

As a teacher and as a person, perhaps better, a person who teaches, distinguishing who I am from what I sometimes do, I am not asked to be perfect. I am only asked to work towards an expansion of awareness of my insecurities and to work towards being increasingly able to be compassionate with them. I would explain compassion as seeing what is, as fully as possible, without judgement. 'Without judgement' is the difficult bit and is at the same time the gateway to awareness.

About this time of the year (February), at least for several years now, I seem to enter a Black Dog period. It is my 'drama queen' month. This period is my reminder of mortality and my embodied experience of why I teach the Blessing of Insecurity, perhaps even my justification for teaching such a subject.

I would say that we all suffer from insecurity, to one degree or another. Mostly we try to get rid of it, or at least mask it. Seldom do we see it as a gift which keeps us on the very edge of presence to who we really are under all our reactivity and disempowerment, which comes from identifying with an accumulation of undigested life experiences. We are not those experiences, but we do so easily allow ourselves to become the victim of them.

There is somewhere a very vivid description of this edge. It is compared to 'licking honey off the edge of a razor blade'. That is exactly what working with Insecurity feels like.

My habit is to be a workaholic. This is not who I am, it is something from which I suffer. When I stick to my practice and meditate a couple of times a day, I am able to spot this suffering instead of just reacting, and can then be a little compassionate with myself and just take all the *shoulds* out of the equation, and I notice what I am doing. In this very noticing, without the conceptualisations, lies the relief: I realise I am meditating, not being driven, and the suffering is no longer there.

When I teach this subject, I am not teaching from a place of superiority, but rather from a place of resonance with all suffering. What is offered is the human being, warts and all, and the students seem to appreciate this. There is resonance; there is joint practice, not didactic. Another chapter will discuss 'the teaching, not the teacher', but this is an introduction to that subject.

When, like many ordinary people, I fall out of practice and suffer a crisis of some kind or another, then it presents a reminder of my inattention and I have a choice again. This is the blessing.

It is so easy to believe that what we feel and think actually comprises who we are. In my head I know I am not that and whatever arises has no intrinsic permanence. I know that and it is fundamental to being able to call oneself a Buddhist, but that is not how it *feels* in the midst of the experience. The reactivity is the disempowerment; the awareness is the detachment from disempowerment.

Let us look for a moment at what Buddhism says about Insecurity. There are just four fundamentals (known as the four Great Seals).

1. All things are impermanent and there is no essential substance or concept that is permanent.
2. All emotions bring pain and suffering and there is no emotion that is purely pleasurable.
3. All phenomena are illusory and empty.
4. Enlightenment is beyond concepts.

Incidentally, Dzonngsar Jamyang Khyentse says about enlightenment that 'it's not a perfect, blissful heaven but rather, a release from delusion'.

Many people have heard of the renowned Four Noble Truths of Buddhism. They are important; they are a wonderful path to living a more focused life; and they are *relative and impermanent* by all the criteria in the Great Seals to which I subscribe.

'The nearest that Buddhism gets to permanence is to say that we hold these statements to be true until someone, scientist or other, can prove them not to be true. If this happens, we will abandon them. After some 2,500 years and more, they remain in place.'

The Dalai Lama

I have described Insecurity as being symptomatic of undigested life experiences that have crystallised into a form that we assume to be our identity. It is that form, that apparently solid identity, that dictates what we teach, what we learn and where we come from when we do either of these things. In order to make any sort of pretence at encouraging the emergence of Spirit, which simply is not an object of the personal intellect but rather its ground, then we must surrender some at least of that which keeps us separate – that very same individual self, which is impermanent.

> In order to live fully,
> I must live on the edge of insecurity.
> This place is dynamic and
> every minute or day that
> I live in that dynamic expands my awareness.
> If I am not expanding
> my awareness, I am dying.
> Blessed are the insecure.
>
> **Mike Boxhall**

In this chapter so far, I have talked about Insecurity and have tried to suggest that it is not a bad thing, but rather an opening to greater awareness. I have also hinted at Impermanence, and have extended that concept, by implication, to Birth.

Here I would like to insert a verbatim conversation between myself and others during a recent course in Italy, which engages with these subjects in a 'live' session. These exchanges were recorded during the opening session of the third and final segment of a three-part course, each part lasting five days. Between them, the contributions touch intimately on the causes of insecurity, the forms that insecurity takes, how we work with insecurity and the blessing of insecurity, when embraced.

Maria: It seems as if these two themes of birth and death are very close together. And for me personally, at this period of time, there have been many questions around birth and death.

Mike: My overall statement about the two of them is that they are not separate. Birth isn't a beginning and death is not an ending. They are stages in a continuum; a continuum of continually coming into form and going back to essence. That, of course, is not always how it feels on an emotional level, which we can call relative or personal.

Maria: Maybe my question is: 'How to stay inside the continual coming and going?'

Mike: I think the answer to that must lie in awareness. That which I call 'I' is not a fixed object, it is an accumulation of experiences. Who is the experiencer of that thing we call I? Perhaps that is closer to the source, but still, necessarily, relative? In other words, I am looking at the word awareness; awareness of birth and death. If I am aware and in the present (which means almost the same thing because to be aware is to be present), the awareness is not being born and is not dying. Being born and dying are the object – the subject is the awareness noticing the coming into being of form.

I suppose the question then is – which we can just leave as a question – 'What dies and what is born?' The difficulty in this is that this discussion is taking place at the level of intellect. The intellect is itself a form, or the lack of intellect, or whatever it may be, which we can observe, so is a feeling. It is a manifestation of what I call Intelligence but that, as I said, is intellectualising about something that is not the intellect. In that sense, all this conversation is reductionist; that is what we do the whole time; remain dualistic.

Inka: I am having a hard time at the moment to express exactly how I am feeling and what I am thinking. I do have a question but I am not sure how to express it. The time since our last seminar has been a very intense period and has been about the integration of my insecurities and how to deal with the pain in my stomach.

Mike: What does that say to you?

Inka: I have been thinking about it a lot. I think there has been some overlapping of different things. I now feel good it is completely over. I still don't feel well inside but I myself feel very well and peaceful.

Mike: So it is possible to have a pain and be peaceful?

Inka: I have experienced at times this possibility of being perfectly present with pain and how that presence would affect my pain and it has been very useful.

Mike: Anything you would like to put in? [addressing someone who hasn't yet spoken]

Yvonne: For me, in this past year, many things have happened and since the last seminar I have opened new pathways.

Mike: Yes, I have seen that in you. I can't quantify it but you seem to have opened new doors.

Yvonne: It's been very chaotic. I haven't been well and I was not well before and although there is chaos in my life, I am very quiet and that is extraordinary.

Mike: I think this is possible and it reflects what Ince was saying about her pain. We cannot get rid of chaos, there is chaos in the universe, it is part of the nature of the universe. But we can develop a form of stillness in observing that chaos without becoming it.

Yvonne: I think so. Things have to develop by themselves and the important thing is to be present – not to protect yourself from being in it but living with it.

Mike: Sure, and somehow not getting too attached. If we struggle to try and get rid of that chaos, whatever and wherever it may be, all we are actually doing is feeding more energy, the energy of awareness, into the chaos.

Yvonne: I also reached a kind of awareness and you will all laugh. I was seven years old when I decided to become a doctor [she did] and now I am 50 years old. Some people tried to make me think I had taken the wrong path at that time, but now I have really become aware of the fact that it has not been wrong. And the other little thing I want to add is that I am sorry for arriving late and that during the meditation I asked for clarity, as that is what I need.

Mike: I think what you have said is very important. Whatever your path is, it is just as good, not better or worse, than anyone else's path. The point is to do it sincerely and nobody else can tell you what your path should be. All paths lead to Rome, as they say chauvinistically in Italy! At the level of the spirit all paths lead to the cause. Medicine is a very fine means of livelihood and it is useful. I had a student in Italy who mends washing machines, which is also a fine livelihood as he does it very sincerely and he is very good at it and it is useful. Teaching craniosacral therapy is a fine livelihood. It is not possible to say one is better than the other. However, one thing you can say is that the spiritual person is the one that does whatever he does from his heart and not just from his head.

Stella: I didn't really feel much like coming here but, on the other hand, I know that coming here is the right thing to do because I stop. It has been an important period of time. I had to assist my mother. She has done well on her own until recently, but I find I have a lot of anger towards my mother. I think I have done well with what I have done with my mother recently and have been able to look at my anger. So I now think that it is a good thing for me to come here and leave her alone for a few days as it means I am liberating myself from chains [obsession].

Mike: Is she aware, or does she suffer from dementia?

Stella: She is aware.

Mike: I mention this because my wife's mother is not aware, at least not at the obvious level. I am convinced, however, that even if people don't have any cognitive thinking left in their head, there is some level of awareness.

Stella: But it's important for me that my mother is aware because that means I cannot tell myself lies. I found out from looking at her that I don't like her very much and this hurts me because she is my mother. That means I have to come here.

Mike: Sure – I think stopping is very useful. If we can stop and be present there is something that is called the eternal present or now. Time is a kind of concept, it was invented by people [that is literally true]. It's a concept. To be able to be present continually is fantastic.

Your mother didn't give you anger. I don't believe one person can give another person anger. It is a human emotion – it's in all of us, as is fear, as is joy. Nobody can give it to you as it's not an object; it's part of the human psyche. This is very difficult: if somebody gives us the opportunity to examine our anger and work with it so that we are not so reactive to it, and it is not so potent – that is a gift.

Stella: In fact I have said this is a very good period of time and I thought of giving thanks.

Mike: Yes I understand – I heard what you said. I am just amplifying it.

Stella: And I never get angry at her, or angry at myself, but I can see her very well.

Mike: Many of us are better at being compassionate with other people than we are with being compassionate with ourselves. Perhaps that is the next stage.

Francesca: It is very difficult for me to say where I am. It has been an intense and emotionally painful period. And there are two things: one thing is that at a certain point I realised that the solution to my pain was getting lost. By that I mean losing all these patterns, habits that came to me. And the other thing is that at a certain point there is a very fine line to getting lost and not finding yourself, and I was scared by that. The only thing I feel like saying right now is that I am getting lost.

Mike: OK. The thing to be considered there is who is the 'I' that is getting lost? And what is getting lost? I haven't got any clever answers, but those are the questions for examination.

Francesca: It's the 'I' I know – my forms, patterns and way of thinking up until now.

Mike: The word that comes to my mind is dissolution. Dissolution of that which in any case has no inherent substance and is a construction.

Laura: In this moment there is a great big chaos. Many things are present at the same moment. The period of time since the last seminar has been very intense and full of things. I am facing the theme of illness and death of people close to me and with this theme going on inside myself, there are questions about the meaning of my life. Many moments I think that what I am doing is not useful, so I doubt my usefulness. Since the last seminar, I have noticed that I do things with more trust and creativity. The other theme is that there are more things about myself that are difficult to accept. I am having a hard time doing everyday tasks, there is some kind of fear when I meet with other people and I have to relate to another person. My life strategy has always been to adapt to the other person and it is very difficult to enquire: 'Who am I? What do I want? What is the path I want to follow?'

Mike: What occurs to me immediately is that everything you said, to some extent, has a down side and an up side. What I think we can focus on is the enormous upside of what you are saying because what you are actually talking about is an increase in awareness of your own process, and from that comes an awareness of an increase in potential in what you can do. By noticing some of your habituations, you have opened the door to not being habituated to them. Does that make sense?

Francesca: Yes.

I should like to close this chapter with a quote from Lewis Carroll:

> 'Who are you?' said the Caterpillar.
>
> This was not an encouraging opening for a conversation. Alice replied, rather shyly, 'I – I hardly know, sir, just at present – at least I know who I was when I got up this morning, but I think I must have been changed several times since then.'
>
> 'What do you mean by that?' said the Caterpillar sternly. 'Explain yourself!'

'I can't explain myself, I'm afraid, sir,' said Alice, 'because I'm not myself, you see.'
'I don't see,' said the Caterpillar.
Alice in Wonderland **Lewis Carroll**

February is sometimes a difficult month; a very difficult one. The following is a reflection on a February of a few years ago.

I think it is worth talking about at least some of the highlights as, whilst we talk a lot about babies and birth elsewhere, we do not talk much about death, which is just as much part of the continuum.

Without going back over every inch of territory between then and now – the memory would, in any case, inevitably be imperfect – I will just concentrate on a few details that remain clear.

When I first became quite obviously ill, I knew I was fragile and sat one morning on the terrace of the place where I was working, looking upstream and contemplating my demise – not for the first time; I have met the horsemen before.

Just in front of me was the place where the spring that feeds this pond arises out of the ancient chalk downs. Home of the original Boxgrove Man and a European Site of Special Scientific Interest.

As I sat, the following came to me:

I have not yet made up my mind.
The stone, the trees, the gently falling hills.
The water, gathered in the folds, to serve the long-quiet Mill.
A place to rest, or sit, it matters not.
I contemplate the source, set in the chalk-white down
From which the water flows;
Cold from the earth but soon to warm;
Enlivened by the mighty sun, which, like a heart,
Quickens the rise and fall of breath.

Fire, earth and water, dance
and take this fragile, mortal form a while;

'till comes the in-breath and tired of this ancient sport,
this separation from the source,
the parts unwind and lifted by the sun, borne by the wind,
fall again into the infinitude of the Mother.
'Look, there's a rainbow!'

Mike Boxhall

There is a story behind the rainbow image which is that during the course of my training in craniosacral therapy at the Karuna Institute, we worked one day on a guided imagery of the experience of our earliest moments, in this case implantation in the womb.

My memory, my 'experience', was of being in a beautiful pale blue sphere, gazing in a state of great happiness at three rainbows. This was eventually clouded by the need to 'get on with life', which I remember perceiving as a pressure from outside, but the first very strong image remains that of the three rainbows. This, then, is my first memory.

It seemed quite appropriate that when I had the sense of dying, one of my last impressions should be of a rainbow.

A rainbow is such an apposite image for both life and death. It is there, very clearly, in the sky, you can even photograph it: but at another level it is a complete illusion. There just is nothing there. It is like a thought or a feeling: it is real at one level, and nothing at another level.

So with our existence. I am real, and yet where am I located? Where is the me who is asking this question? There is such a difference between asking this question philosophically or intellectually and asking it from emptiness.

Shortly after writing this poem, I flew to Florida and taught a five-day course at the lovely Atlantic Centre for the Arts, Smyrna Beach. The course went well – and then I energetically crashed on the last day after flying from Orlando to Miami International.

The thing that was extraordinary over the next few weeks was the witnessing of this rainbow-like intangibility, especially in Florida where I gave up on further voyaging for that moment. Right at the check-in for a flight to the Galapagos Islands, I just stood there and realised that I could not go any further and expect to arrive in the same form. I just stayed in Florida with kind friends, who were incidentally a three-hour bus ride away from the airport, and watched my whole being and all its parts unwind for a week. Disintegration in a most literal sense. It was like an atomic destructuring. Much tiredness, no particular fear, then a gradual restructuring. How or why, I do not know. There must have been some rain and the ephemeral re-formed.

The colours are bright, but really there is nothing there that is separate. I have long known this, but the experience is to be treasured. A strange chapter, this, but I wanted to write it and it has been very difficult.

9
The Tide

My thesis, my conviction (not just belief) and my passion are contained in this short phrase: 'You can rely upon the tide.' I have spent the last 15–20 years analysing, testing, working with and then teaching the truth of that statement.

Today, 120 years or so after Sutherland first voiced that statement, I am going to try to explain where I have been and what I have come up with, so far. And I am going to ask you to experience a flavour of that over the course of the next few pages.

Let's take this slowly and start at the beginning. I first heard this phrase when I was training in craniosacral therapy with Franklyn Sills at Karuna.

'You can rely upon the tide.' I began to think, 'What tide, and what does "rely on" mean?' The word 'rely' was the big one. Did 'rely' mean work with, manipulate in some way, or direct at a lesion? Why did Sutherland choose that expression? I came to believe that he was independent enough to know what he meant and that he meant 'rely' literally. That means someone else or something else does it, whatever is to be done.

I came to believe that he was talking about the hypothesis that there is an Intelligence that is not part of the individual and personal ego structure, not subject to the Intellect, which can be absolutely relied upon.

Shakespeare said, 'There is a tide in the affairs of men, which taken at the flood, leads on to fortune.' Even that is not it, but it is a shade closer. It implies an 'other'.

This raises a big conflict. If there is an 'other' that can be relied on, what place is there for me? How will I know what it is doing? How will I know what is happening to the patient? Supposing something goes wrong and I get sued – what a litigious country this is! You see what is happening here: the poor old personal ego is having a bad time already, getting really anxious. We could go on further. 'We have to have boundaries, I can't not know what I am doing. How do I explain what I am doing? It's not scientific and best of all, I have got to be present, fully present, at all times!'

Oh, boy! Now nobody can be trusted, not even me!

It's not that bad. What we need to do now is have a look at what being present means in this context.

What I mean by being present is to be mentally still, just noticing what arises without getting attached to it in any way. Without making any judgements about what something *means*. Just noticing that it is. If we don't get attached to meaning, the phenomenon will pass and another will most likely take its place. Then another and another and they are all acknowledged and all let go of and sometimes, just for a while, nothing will arise and there is just empty awareness, empty of all objects, and from that emptiness a new object arises.

Movement arises out of stillness and nothing truly *goes* anywhere. It just is, in movement. There is a coming together in this moment of everything that ever was and this is its expression right now. The Spirit takes form and we as witness are in joint practice with that form.

That's the introduction, the prologue; now let's unpick this a little and break it down into something a little more expansive.

All objects come and go, don't they? Some take longer to go than others. Everest, the planet, my hard-rock-playing neighbour, but sooner or later they all go and that is what all things and thoughts and feelings have in common. They all go. I shall go, I don't know when, perhaps I have outlived my sell-by date, but I shall go. And this is the most important bit: whatever came into form as me will come into form as something else, or part of something else, sooner or later.

When the conditions support another form, another form will be there. No beginning, no end. No cause, just revelation.

I can't help laughing at myself for trying to be logical. It is not what I do best. I think that in Jung's model I am probably an intuitive, at least that is my intuition, but try I must if I am not to remain lopsided.

My logic is that the more I can objectivise everything, including myself, the closer I am to the unexpressed, the non-dual, that out of which all objects arise. The subject.

Where I am leading to is that if everything is, in a sense, not concrete and is impermanent, including myself, then so is impairment, illness, suffering and disease. If this is the case, then what tool am I going to use to effect ease?

Patently my intellect, not only impermanent, but also limited, can only hold a partial answer. That is, of course, unless I claim to be omniscient and know everything. The best I can do, in this form, is to take my limited knowledge and apply it to my limited assessment, call it diagnosis and hope for a limited beneficial result.

Further rambling around this thought leads me to realise that, so often, even the client does not actually know the cause of what is wrong with her. That compounds the problem

That's what we work with the whole time, though, isn't it?

We are conditioned, I believe, to think that we do have to know what is wrong.

Nowadays, I have a slightly different point of view, not as an absolute, but I offer it as an invitation to consider that there is possibly a different perspective to examine.

Sometimes, in fact, everything is perfectly satisfactory, if we can look at things a little differently.

Suppose I just get out of the way and let the Spirit or the Intelligence, as opposed to my intellect, do the work. Get the pathology of the system back into a better adapted state, no longer suffering from what are, in effect, undigested life experiences. It would be super-intelligent to let Intelligence do the work instead of relying just on my intellect and partial knowledge.

That would, in my view, open the possibility of rebirth, right now, in the present into a form no longer modified by my undigested life. It is my belief and, to some extent, experience that rebirth is not just about what happens when I fall off my twig, but rather more, combined with awareness, what is happening right now, in the present. As Aldous Huxley said, 'In actuality, there is no life outside the life of experience.' Let us revere the experience, not just the theory or the concept.

There is a lovely pod of people that has grown around a course I taught in North Carolina. We exchange a lot of questions and we exchange a lot of attempts at answers. It is very much a joint practice. Some of what follows stemmed out of a recent question from one member to us all, and my reply to that question.

Let's focus for a moment on the oil disaster in the Gulf of Mexico and see what arises directly out of that. As well as being a disaster, which it is, for hundreds of thousands of good people – it is almost unbearable to think of the suffering of those who have lost everything; family, homes, possessions and, worse, hope and trust – it is a global crisis. Focused on New Orleans.

A crisis is a turning point. I am not just talking about the price of oil and the snowball effect that has, but a crisis of trust in what we come to believe in as being the natural order of things. Even so far as a crisis of trust in the truth of decency and compassion and neighbourliness when the chips are down, for some people.

The crisis that has gone around the world is the question of who we can rely on when we are in trouble.

I believe 9/11 was different: we created an enemy and took the view that we had to learn to defend ourselves better from the enemy, that object out there. We rallied around to do that. Rightly or wrongly.

Now it seems that we have been betrayed by ourselves. There is no enemy out there – though we shall look for one – just a massive indictment of a way of life lacking compassion.

I would not pretend that I would expect any different result from any other nation should a similar situation arise. Certainly not from my own, which is inexorably cast in the same model, as are all European countries. Just before the hurricane, there were over 600 people trampled to death in Arabia, mostly women and children fleeing in panic from a perceived threat to themselves. If I were an historian, the list would be endless.

Now we come to the crisis, the turning point. The fulcrum for change.

That fulcrum lies in awareness. Not the awareness of who did what wrong and who needs firing or blaming, but the awareness that I am responsible.

Historically, we always blame someone else and go back to surrendering to the impulse of accepting what is best for me and mine, as though the rest of the world community were not also me and mine.

The status quo gets rocked. No wonder we are 'experiencing some major shifts and upheavals in our lives'.

Daniel Levy, a composer and pianist, says:

> The steps to attain patterns of a new civilisation are the same as those for the expansion of consciousness. When this expansion of consciousness occurs the whole past gradually and rhythmically diminishes to become part of a new whole. The centre changes and each of our atoms is infused with a different sort of energy. Our point of view assumes a growing perspective and our vision expands from seeing parts of the whole to an awareness of the reality of the greater whole.

This is, succinctly, the experience of some clients. This is sometimes my experience. 'Something happened', as Rollin Becker DO (a renowned American osteopath) would say.

'God is a circle whose centre is everywhere and whose circumference is nowhere,' said St Bonaventure, a Franciscan cardinal of the thirteenth century and the patron saint of bowel disorders. Not too many people know that!

To put it another way, 'The Buddha of the future is Maitreya. But Maitreya is not a person but the quality of friendship that is, in fact, an aspect of enlightened mind' (Deena Metzger).

This is where our work is so important. Not that we tell other people how they should be or what they should do, but that we facilitate access to awareness of what is coming up in our own beings right now and bring that into fuller acuteness. And we remove the judgement. We do this in joint practice with another or others and we help them to come into presence with their pain, of whatever nature, by hearing fully their story from an empty place.

Only by and from this increase in awareness will the possibility for root change arise. All important change causes Insecurity. If we are not insecure we are skating round the same old rut and there may be an artificial and temporary sense of security in that, but look how fragile it is! So the insecurity is the place of change. Blessed are the insecure. The pain will change if we can watch it, not become it, not let it become who we are. In that full hearing lies the healing. There is nothing to do. But it is not easy to be fully present to deep anguish without judgement. We just have to remember that this judgement is our stuff and it is filling the bowl and if the bowl is not empty, the whole story does not get told.

Going back to blame for a moment, the question is not 'What did I do wrong?' but what comes up right now. What does what I did or didn't do feel like right now? Is it anger, is it fear, is it a mixture of both? That is what needs taking on board and working with. Out of that comes the possibility for change. Work with the fear, work with the anger, and if I can do that then, just maybe, I will see the anger and/or the fear to be a common human condition and I will not have to defend myself against it in future, or get rid of it.

It is basically fear, fear of change, which in turn means fear of being, and that makes us so pathological.

To have fear is part of the human experience; the problem is when we try to create conditions, barriers and defences which guard us against it. This is when we seize up.

Let's work *with* the fear, if that is what is there. Then we are in the present. From the present we can make sensible decisions. The present is always still, it is what we are observing that is changing. So we are still, watching the arising and falling of phenomena. We are not the phenomena. We are, in that moment, the place where all phenomena arise.

That is what stillness means. It is not an inert state; it is the awareness of change, not the change itself. It leads to proactivity. Being caught up (attached) to the change leads to reactivity.

I have tried to define Stillness and I have tried to define non-attachment. The combination of the two is enlightenment. Any fool, including this one, can define it – to *practise* it is the ballgame!

Nietzsche said – and he could have been speaking of attachment, or rather the lack of it – 'I want to learn more and more to see as beautiful what is necessary in things, then I shall be one of those who make things beautiful.'

For a few years now I have been sharing my observations with students, both in the USA and in Europe. They have been sharing their observations with me and the consensus is, 'You can rely upon the tide.' Not the mechanical, relatively surface tides, so much – they are a tool, a vehicle – but the Breath of Life, the Intelligence, that they carry and the Spirit, of which the Breath of Life is an early form.

A further consensus is that it is difficult to enter that state of surrender, where the poor old ego cannot circumscribe what is going on. It does want to have its say! The final consensus is that when the reliance, the trust, the surrender is in place, nothing less, it works!

The secret, for me, is in our state of presence. The Dalai Lama says, 'I think that our first responsibility as practitioners is to watch ourselves.' I note the use of 'first responsibility'.

I have to do something a little more than just washing my hands between patients and having a cup of tea. I need to meditate and come into a state of being which is relatively unattached. If I cannot be unattached, then a simple observation of that fact can disentangle me from being the attachment, to a point that I can just observe the state of my being, without putting the energy of attention into the neurosis, or whatever there may be. I have plenty of those. This observation without judgement is compassion – Karuna. Whenever I can approach someone from this relatively uncluttered, relatively still place, I am ready to receive what is offered.

I do not expect absolute emptiness. I think I may have had brief glimpses of something like it from time to time, but with an amount of practice I can be relatively still.

From there, and from there only, I can approach the client or the family group, if I am working with minors or babies, in the belief that I will contact that level in whoever is present, whether it comes into awareness or not.

We are then in joint practice, at that level, and whatever arises, whatever gets done, is the result of the synergy of that joint practice. There is no doer and no done-to. There is only the joint practice. And I may not know what has taken place, at a structural level, and the client may not know, and both those are scary, but it is perfect – and who is scared? Not me, only my ego!

There is, unfortunately, no half falling off a cliff. You either trust and let go, or you don't.

I know some people are drawn to work like this. I know some people are repelled by the thought of working like this. They are both right. I just want to empower the former in any way I can.

This to me is the level of the Spirit. It is not a better level; it is what is, for some people.

> A dog loves the world through its nose.
> A fish through its gills.
> A bat through its deep sense of blindness.
> An eagle through its glide.
> And a human life
> through its spirit.
>
> *Look Around*, Mark Nepo

I have not proved anything. I did not set out to. I wanted to make an offering.

Mark Nepo, again, quotes the Buddha: 'Act always as if the future of the Universe depends on what you do, while laughing at yourself for thinking that whatever you do makes any difference.'

Let me finish with one man's definition of craniosacral therapy:

'Craniosacral therapy, at its tenderest, is a journey taken in stillness by two or more people towards a level of being where there is no pathology' (M.B.).

The following from Christina in Switzerland touches very much on the concept of 'undigested life experience' mentioned earlier. It addresses very well the fact that if we go deep enough into the core of relationship – what is sometimes called joint practice – the synergy arising from that field will, without any effort or even intention, allow a 'rebirth'. Let the work do the work. We need only sit in awe of the revelation. I am very grateful for this contribution.

> Dear Mike
> You asked us to write something on the work we do at Duncton Mill – at least this is what I understood.
>
> After the last two courses I have had a difficult time with myself. I found it hard to adjust to 'regular life', a life where I had to make the decisions when to do what, as I am not employed nor have a full practice. I have questioned many of my decisions taken previously, and wondered if I had missed my task in life or gone off it – and all those most unpleasant thoughts and questionings. It seemed to me I needed to do much 'digesting' – not only of old life experiences that had accumulated throughout the decades, beliefs that evolved out of them (or I made out of them), but also of the experiences in your courses.
>
> Only in the last few days have I started to realise that experiences and resulting beliefs are starting to change; quite imperceptively, actually.
>
> During the 'morning musings' and the sharing of our experiences of our work together, the concept of 'undigested life experiences' comes up every so often, as the source of our physical, emotional, mental or spiritual discomfort or dis-ease. However, very seldom do any of us share or talk about a very specific experience that we have not digested yet, the way one often seems to do in psychotherapy. And yet, those up to that moment

in time undigested life experience seems to start digesting itself. Simply, if that is not too modest a word to use, by connecting to another person from a deep, compassionate and non-judgemental place.

If I may use the analogy of 'digesting' in a more physical way: if we eat something that is hard to digest, our body either stores it in fat or other unhealthy cells or the lump in the stomach moves forward very slowly and painfully. If we drink some healthful herbal tea that helps digestion or another remedy, the stomach and intestines start working much better and start clearing out the unhealthy stuff. And if we add some herbal or homeopathic remedies (remedies that do not burden the body in other ways) to strengthen let's say the kidney and liver function, the body may start clearing out even older 'poisons' and become well.

That is how I experience the work we do on courses. The deep listening in joint practice is like beneficial herbal tea or homeopathic remedy, enabling or strengthening the body, soul and spirit to heal, to digest what needs to be healed first and then to go deeper and deeper into the cell tissue.

That last sentence would actually lead me to muse about 'healing the spirit'. Maybe I ought to capitalise the S in spirit when writing about the universal Spirit, because He/She does not need any healing, to distinguish them from the personal spirit that may very well need plenty of healing.

And now, of course, must follow a few thoughts about healing, as this is not really a word you use, as far as I am aware of. Much more it seems to me you speak about 'shedding light' on what is, accepting it more and more without judgement, with compassion, will bring healing, maybe not in the conventional sense of getting 'healthy', but becoming clear with what is.

This way of working with others reminds me also of how little children react when they hurt themselves and cry. If we as parents simply hug them and acknowledge, 'oh yes, I see you hurt so much', they cry even louder, but for only a second or two, and then it usually seems OK. (When on the other hand someone says to a hurt child 'oh, it's not so bad, it's nothing', they cry and sniffle for very much longer.) As a therapist I am like the parent, acknowledging and validating what happened and how it feels, and then 'it' can dissolve.

As a parent it makes me feel good within myself to be loving and accepting of a child. As a therapist, if I am connecting from a deep place to the client, I am of course connecting to myself from that same deep place, accepting, allowing the light to shine onto whatever is. I have experienced again and again that giving a treatment is receiving a treatment.

> Before the birth of Heaven and Earth, there was something without form but complete. Silent. Empty. Independent. Unchanging. Infinite. Eternal. It is the Mother of all things. I cannot classify it, but I call it Dao. Powerful, it creates all things, is present in all things, returns all things to their origin. The Dao is great. Heaven is great. Earth is great. Humanity is great. These are the four great things. Humanity follows Earth. Earth follows Heaven. Heaven follows Dao. Dao follows its own nature.
>
> (This is a Daoist quotation but it parallels the confessions of St Augustine who had to say that there was something before God – the formless.)

A word about models: Buddhism, Christianity, Judaism, philosophy, psychology and indeed craniosacral therapy are all models. They are not it. Any of them is only it when it becomes an experience at a deep level. In the meantime we are talking about theories, models, thoughts, opinions, dreams, hopes and prayers about the experience. This is a pretty dogmatic statement and I hate dogma, so I will modify it by adding, *in the opinion of many people whose judgement I respect.*

The next piece of dogma (which carries the same modification) is that the deepest levels are formless and are not subject to the intellect, which, like thoughts and emotions, never mind the body itself, is already form. We could call these levels the Spirit, the universal that comes into individual and infinite variety of form. I often refer to this as Intelligence, *the* Intelligence as differentiated from one of its products, which is the personal Intellect.

Let us not confuse the Spirit, which I see as being absolute, whether expressed or imminent, with the Soul, which I see as being personal and another product of the infinite Spirit.

To touch, to become, the Intelligence itself, even for a moment, is to touch that which causes formation and can lead to rebirth, in the present, right now, back into form that may no longer carry the accumulations of disempowering life experience, referred to above.

Medicine, in general, may be said to be linear and Newtonian: all that happened had a definite cause and gave rise to a definite effect (Capra). That is to say, the world was a clockwork. Tick led inexorably to tock.

In the last thirty years or so, the decisive change in the West has been to recognise that nature is relentlessly non-linear (Stewart). What does that mean? It means, in my interpretation, that we cannot just use our intellects to rationalise sequences of cause and effect, or diagnosis and prognosis and remedy, if we are to reach levels of being other than those subject to the laws governing small bodies, i.e. relatively uncomplicated bodies. That in turn means that the structure, the form of the human being, is subject perhaps to linear interpretation, but that the Infinite aspects are not.

Ants and bees have individual intelligence, although not very great, but the same creatures have a large group intelligence which allows them to do extraordinary things.

There are laws governing small things and there are laws governing big things. When we have finished dissecting small things and irreducibly arrive at the no thing, we have arrived at the biggest thing of all, the Intelligence, the Infinite.

You might like this little piece that I wrote a while back. I believe it nicely illustrates what we are talking about.

Potatoes

Spring is coming, believe me, it always does, in whatever form it chooses to take and I look forward to a period of enormous activity in my vegetable plot.

Traditionally early potatoes go in on Easter Monday. That is, of course, if it is not raining or snowing or if the ground is not too hard or too soft or indeed, if I am not in bed with some sort of flu!

It seemed like a good time to think about habit and consider just how much of our lives are driven by it.

By and large potatoes know when to grow and how to grow. They have potato intelligence. All we need to do is provide them with the space and conditions in which to grow. We do not know how to grow a potato; we only know how to facilitate its being a potato.

I wonder how many of our difficulties in the work come from our thinking that we do have to know?

Somehow a cure, a state of balanced being can only happen if I have enough knowledge.? This would only be true and possible if I had all knowledge.

The other way perhaps, is to rely on the potato's intelligence. It knows!

I think that we sometimes get too involved with the method to the detriment of being in touch with the essence, which is not method or even any of the tides but the intelligence that they carry, as a temple contains the Spirit. The tides are not IT, the essence is IT.

How scary it is to give up the security of knowing but only by giving up the Personal, which is knowing can we reach the Transpersonal, which is Essence.

I should be happy to work with anyone who wants this insecurity. I have plenty to offer to the debate! In the meantime my potatoes are in the dark, beginning to push out their first blind but intelligent shoots.

(Mike Boxhall)

When the human intellect, which is a small thing, wrestles with the meaning of the Big Thing, it arrives at a point where it is trying to be separate from Infinity. This is an impossibility.

The Intellect, while it is separate from Intelligence itself, has reached its limit. To go further, it must give up its separateness, let go and become its own cause. There is no extrapolation from the Infinite.

I have been accused of getting dangerously close to perpetuating the Cartesian split in these separations of Intelligence and Intellect and, as I have repeated similar statements several times, I need to say that I am not talking about two different things, but rather about two degrees or levels of Intelligence – that which is mine, personal and egoic, and that which is infinite, unconfined and common to all life.

I am the tide

The story of Adam and Eve is the story of gaining individuality and losing unity, unity with the Infinite.

It is the experience of some of us that if we are prepared to accept the ultimate and terrifying loss of individual self-awareness, it becomes possible to become the Spirit, Intelligence, the Tide itself. This is terrifying because, again by definition, we cannot know that. There is only the void, which is not an object, just an experience of no thing, with no form until we return to relative awareness. There is, of course, no terror in the void – that is in the letting go, the falling off the cliff. There is no pain, pleasure or sickness either; there is no life experience, which causes all these phenomena.

There are – shock, horror! – no boundaries. They have not come into existence yet. There is just void.

If we forget about this journey being linear, but think of it rather as a journey into the very heart of who we are, then it may be seen that the possibility of emergence into the relative contains the possibility of not carrying with us the pathology which is from a linear projection, whether from the past or into the future.

I do not believe in miracles. I do believe that trauma, of whatever nature, is an accumulation of past or future events. Under every pathology, and all the events that led to that pathology, is a present health.

Let us work with the health, which is the core, rather than the pathology, which is in a sense peripheral.

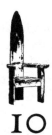

10

Form and Emptiness

What I have learned from Milarepa (a Tibetan rogue who became a saint of the eleventh century CE) is that when I don't like what arises, I try not to get rid of it but rather get to know it better by 'schmoozing' it. Offering tea with finely cut cucumber sandwiches would be the English way, but 'schmoozing' will do.

It is not my job to teach how to manufacture objects. Much of my work is very subjective. It is almost impossible to have a 'this is how it is' approach to the Spirit. On the other hand, in the 'real world' many objects that come into our lives nowadays are accompanied by instruction manuals which tell us how to assemble them. It is unfortunate that many of these manuals are written in a language which apparently was learned without the aid of an instruction manual, but be that as it may, there is an inference that if the instructions are not followed, the object will not take its required form. That seems very valid for objects.

Once we have learned the instructions and have successfully built an example, we can safely assume that the process will work for everyone who can follow the instructions.

This, I suggest, does not apply to spiritual work, as each person's path will be mediated by a different life experience. There cannot be an embodied experience of the absolute, whatever form you see that as taking, by walking someone else's path.

For this reason I get cross with some of the dogmatic approaches of both Christianity and Buddhism. 'It is said . . .' is followed by a long speech, evidencing a massive feat of memory but with no reference to time, place or space. On the one hand, this is not an embodied experience but a concept, and on the other hand, it reifies the original experience, that of the first proposer of the tract, and turns a felt sense, a genuine mystical experience, into a commodity or dogma.

> Monasteries are like collecting-station for hollow drift.
> The priestly life is deceptive and illusory to me. Of such prisons I have no need.
>
> **Milarepa**

It seems to me that both Jesus and the Buddha exemplified that life must be lived: embodied, not conceptualised in feats of memory about other people's lives. I believe that neither of them made much reference to other people's lives. They were too busy being present.

It is very important that we do not regard spirituality as a thing, an object that is somehow 'out there'. I see spirituality as being, rather, an experience of being the truth of one's life.

I like this quotation from Jack Kornfield on the subject:

> **What happens to most pieces of truth**
>
> One day Mara, the Buddhist god of ignorance and evil, was travelling through the villages of India with his attendants. He saw a man doing walking meditation whose face was lit up in wonder. The man had just discovered something on the ground in front of him. Mara's attendants asked what that was and Mara replied, 'A piece of truth.' 'Doesn't this bother you when someone finds a piece of the truth, O evil one?' his attendants asked. 'No,' Mara replied. 'Right after this they usually make a belief out of it.'

And this from Christina Feldman and Jack Kornfield, in 'Stories of the Spirit, Stories of the Heart', from *Everyday Mind*, edited by Jean Smith, a *Tricycle* book.

> I want to go further and say that whatever state that the human being is capable of realizing, is already in place, present, inherent and the natural state. The work to be undergone therefore, is the awareness expanding into the embodied awareness. Without the embodiment, we remain with the concept.

We are not come together in this writing to learn how to do something. We are not developing more amazing techniques in some therapy. We are on a voyage of discovery of who it is that is doing the work, and what it is that separates us from the source of everything. It is a voyage, first of all, into the Health which is at the core of all of us. And from that place of Health, and I might say beauty, to approach that same place in the other that we may call client, friend, family, or even enemy. So that they bring to their awareness the Health that lies at their heart, centre or core, whatever you want to call it.

So that is our journey – I might say it is essentially a journey without end. Why is it a journey without end? Because it is a journey to a realisation of that which is infinite.

Thomas Merton, *Conjectures of a Guilty Bystander*, wrote:

> The things we really need, come to us only as gifts, and in order to receive them as gifts we have to be open. In order to be open we have to renounce ourselves, in a sense we have to die to our image of ourselves, our autonomy, our fixation upon our self-willed identity. We have to be able to relax the psychic and spiritual cramp which knots us in the painful, vulnerable, helpless 'I' that is all we know as ourselves.

Recently, on a course that I was conducting with advanced level therapists, one remarked that it was his observation that a direct transmission (by this he meant that he perceived that a communication was taking place at a non-verbal or direct mind to mind level or, as I would prefer, the level of heart to heart) was taking place. His actual words were, 'You are giving a direct transmission, aren't you?'

My immediate reaction was to deny this hotly and distance myself from any possibility that I thought or intended any such thing. Inflation! Horror!

Having got some of the chatter of my ego out of the way, as that is what we are talking about, I am able to see a slightly different picture.

I have worked with a few more groups since then and, with the trace of that thought implanted somewhere in the back of my mind, I realise that when two or more people are working together in joint practice, at a deep level, there is indeed a transmission – but it is not from ego to ego but rather from the third presence, which is created at this level of relationship, onto all the other parties. There is a resonance here with Jung's concept of the 'chymical' wedding and the birth of the *puer aeternatus*. There is no doing, only an exchange of being. My observation is that the awareness of the process as a concept may be held by the practitioner, or by the practitioner and the patient, or even by neither. The work is done by the *work* that is created, not by the personality of the participants. I also observe that while the work remains at this level and 'happens', and as the systems are homoeostatic, it is safe.

Something happens. How the body's experience of the event is translated later by the patient or the practitioner into language will depend on factors such as culture, age, gender, state of health, etc. of the two individuals.

At this level the work can be truly transformative and results from the intelligence of one joining with the intelligence of the other, to allow a third and greater intelligence which operates with a precision far beyond the capacity of the intellect. I see no overt action, only the remembrance of the original matrix and opportunity to let go of the accumulations of life experience – undigested – that this brings. It is worth repeating that the subject is not the practitioner, but rather the third. I call this third 'the Spirit'. The Spirit is not a product of the ego.

This dynamic can be correspondingly more powerful in a group of more than two if the withdrawal of intention to do is withdrawn by all the parties and only the intention to hear or follow is in place.

Perhaps we might better say, 'when only the intention to be present to what is, is in place'.

> 'I think, therefore I am,' is the famous phrase coined by René Descartes. This has become the motto of the modern mind. Descartes championed the mind-matter split. Since then, Western science, philosophy and education have been based on the subject-object divide and the human-nature divide. Much of our social and political paradigm stems from this dualism.
>
> From this dualism flow individualism, industrialism, humanism, capitalism and egoism. Dualism also gives birth to fragmentation, separation, alienation and isolation.
>
> (Satish Kumar in *Resurgence*, issue 199)

I lay no claims to being a seer, but it seems possible that the end of the second millennium and the beginning of the third may well become known as the post-Descartian, post-Cartesian era, if you will, and the beginning of the rebirth of Wisdom. It is perhaps time for Knowledge, as differentiated from Information. We are stuffed with information, but information is always *about* something and implies a separation from the object. This separation leads to alienation, judgement and a doing of something to, or sometimes for, the object, based entirely on incomplete information. Because it is incomplete, it is therefore false.

To be sure, the last days of overweening superiority of the Intellect will not be bloodless. The ego will not quietly allow a co-dependence with another. The paradox of the ego is that we cannot get rid of it. Who would be the subject and who would be the object? What we can do is to enlighten it. Know it and work with it. Thus we become whole and real.

What I think, and certainly hope, is that we are working towards a realisation of the *co*-dependence of ourselves, the planet and everything in and on it. Life may become a joint practice in which I realise that 'I am because we are' (a South African perspective). This, roughly, is the message of Deep Ecology, one of the latest and most comprehensive sciences, in my opinion. It is a science which seems to be truly searching for a unification practice, not just a theory.

We have discussed elsewhere that doing less is more. We have gone further and said that doing nothing, just being, with the only intentionality being to hear, receive, accept, acknowledge, validate, is sufficient. These values, lumped together, I call 'trust'. In this acceptance of who we are, we remember who we are *meant* to be and are in the possibility of rebirth into that intention. Intelligence is contacted. To contact this intelligence, which is universal, may mean sinking into awareness which is below the intellect.

I am told we *need* to do more than enter the stillness of awareness. I have no judgement about that need. I make the observation that it is not necessary, just a need! The need can then be accepted like all other manifestations of the intellect. Stillness is not an escape from anything, it is a dynamic process which allows the whole to come into unfoldment. It is not easy to hold and involves practice in being in the present without the rabbiting of the past and the future. It is one way to go.

Trust the tide, or whatever you call that energy. It will take you there. Only, you have to trust it!

If you have to know what is going on, then you are reducing the possibilities.

The following are a few notes taken verbatim from a course held recently beside Lake Garda in Italy. The venue was a Buddhist centre and the extracts may serve to illustrate from 'real' experiences some of the concepts outlined above.

Claudia: I had this release, it felt as if something came out of me that had been stopping me being myself. It seemed to be something like a spirit that came out of me. Other things have happened, but this was the most important aspect of the session.

Inka: Claudia is sharing something that I did not want to share but now I will. At one moment I really understood the significance of love.

Mike: Why didn't you want to share that?

Inka: I know it's important, but I wanted to keep it to myself.

Mike: I thought it was perhaps something like that. The important thing is that if we try to hang onto things we lose them. Sooner or later we lose. On the other hand, if we freely give them away they come back a thousand times. What they say in Christianity is: 'Cast your bread upon the waters.'

Inka: It's true, but I am having a hard time to put this into words.

Mike: It is very difficult, but the purpose of this group, for all of us, is to share ourselves not just our goodies; not just our sweets. To share our difficulties and our humanity. That is the big gift that we can give each other. The tendency that we all have is to make sure that what we give the other person is beautifully wrapped and nicely sanitised. The real gift is to give ourselves just as we are.

Inka: We were talking about this difficulty of putting things into words. I told Claudia that there is no need for her to understand. We agreed that words change things and they don't often show things the way they are. I am not justifying myself but, in this case, I thought I would ruin the experience with words. [We all know that one, don't we?]

Mike: Yes, that can happen – I am going to take a risk and I am going to go one stage further. It often happens with me, that if I try to describe something that I know is not my experience, it becomes a description of an experience, not the actual event. However, there may be some resonance within the other person, not of the same event, but a comparable sensitivity in themselves. So I may have given the other person something – that is a gift – it may not be the same as my experience. And it may be that whatever they have received is an important experience for them. The only risk of loss is to my own ego that wants to hang on to that feeling. That is why I said it is worth trying, because your intentionality is to give a gift to the universe and the only possibility of loss is to that artificial condition that we call 'Me'. Does that make sense to you, Inka?

Inka: Yes. It's very clear.

Mike: So, in Mahayana Buddhism, which this place is a part of, they have a tradition of the *bodhisattva*. A *bodhisattva* is an enlightened being who chooses to keep on coming back into form as a person, so that he or she can help others find their illumination until everyone is illuminated. In effect, to take that vow of becoming a *bodhisattva* is to take a vow for ever. To keep on and on being reborn in order to be of service to other people; which means giving and giving and giving. The only thing you have to give which is truly your own is your own enlightenment, and even that you have to give away. So you see what I am trying to say to you. If you hang on to your own enlightenment you are irrevocably attached. Give it to your friends. It will probably come back. OK. Good, thank you.

Another day:

Mike: There is another very important teaching and it goes something like this. We cannot get what we really need by waiting for it to be given to us. We have to ask for it. Demand it. Take it. Do I make any sense here? Whether we are talking about liberation, or whatever you want to call it, there is no freedom if we are given freedom. All we are getting then is a debt to the person who is giving us freedom.

Question: Can you repeat or rephrase that?

Mike: Let me continue with this point for just a moment, as it is very important. If somebody takes off our chains we are not free because we are in debt to them for ever. Does this make any sense to anyone, as it's a very tricky area, this? If you see little birds, they sit there with their mouths open and Mummy comes along and pushes some worms into them. That is normal with babies and children. But it only addresses physical growth – you could say it is mechanical and is concerned with the nourishment of the body, but not the nourishment of the spirit. If we are not going to be chained to the dogmatic teaching, freedom needs somehow to be taken . . .

Translator: Sorry, what needs to be taken? I didn't understand.

Mike: Spiritual growth. Otherwise we are putting on another chain of debt. This is why I say, 'What would be useful or what do you need?' That way you are getting in touch with your own expanded awareness; awareness of lack or need, rather than waiting for the teacher to pass on another 10,000 words that he has learned by heart and which originally applied to another person's experience in another time, place and cultural relevance.

If, on the other hand, we just listen to repetitive teachings we are only getting what the teacher needs to give us. It's a joint practice between the two. That's why I keep saying at the beginning of each course: 'What do you need?' 'What would be useful?'

There is just one Truth and there are ten thousand million people on the planet. I haven't counted them recently and every time I do somebody else gets born. So there is just one Truth, so for however many different people there are on the planet there are that number of different ways of realising the Truth. That's why I say: 'What question comes up for you?'

You see what I've done now is made everybody think [laughter], whereas before I started that, everybody was cruising along quite nicely thinking nothing was going to be disturbing; I can look forward to five days' rest without a computer or a telephone or cooking or shopping or driving or looking after other people.

Maria: It seems as if the two themes of birth and death are very close together. And for me personally, at this period of time, there have been many questions around birth and death.

Mike: My overall statement about the two of them is that they are not separate. Birth isn't a beginning and death is not an ending. They are mere stages in a continuum; a continuum of continually coming into form and going back to essence.

That, of course, is not always how it feels on an emotional level.

Maria: Maybe my question is: 'How to stay inside the continual coming and going?'

Mike: I think the answer to that must lie in awareness. That which I call 'I' is not a fixed object, it is a set of relationships, of experiences. Who is the experiencer? In other words I am looking at the word awareness; awareness of birth and death. If I am aware and in the present (which means almost the same thing because to be aware is to be present), the awareness is not being born and is not dying. Being born and dying are the object – the subject is the awareness taking form and losing form. I suppose the question, then – which we can just leave as a question – is: 'What dies and what is born?'

The difficulty in this is that this discussion is taking place at the level of intellect. The intellect is itself a form which we can observe, or the lack of intellect, or whatever it may be; so is a feeling. It is a manifestation of what I call Intelligence but that, as I said, is intellectualising about something that is not the intellect. In that sense, all this conversation is reductionist; that is what we do the whole time; remain dualistic.

II

Change

Change is such an important subject for our consideration. It is, perhaps, the only constant in the universe and paradoxically, the bedrock of our existence. There is no birth or death; no coming, no going, no thinking, feeling, sensation or intuition; no relationship, of any nature, without change.

This me is not the me I was (or had) yesterday. The more I practise being in the present, the more obvious this becomes. There was a time when I knew exactly who I was. My job, my family, my bank balance (or overdraft), my clubs, my teams, my clothes, my schools, my conversation, my politics, my neuroses, all served to identify this being. Not always comfortable, I might say, but clearly identified.

There was a later time when, with a rather painful shift in awareness, there was a me in relationship to other beings, places, environments and situations. A sort of more co-operative being that took some responsibility for causing waves as well a being a victim of them.

There comes now another time, which is beyond all understanding, as far as I am concerned, where I just do not know who this being is, in continuous stretches at any rate. Sometimes yes, there is a me operating but then, there are other times, when I can only listen to what is being said, or imagined, by the saying or the imagining. The confusion only subsides when the analysis subsides and is replaced with surrender.

This surrender is at its extreme when I am teaching embodiment, in groups, and the work is going very deep as the work becomes a synergy of the whole group. Then there is trust and I can let go. What is let go is the separation, the personal, the abstracted – the work does the work and there is no other doer. There is no doer! There is no me. There is a powerful sense of the teaching being the only clarity in a disintegrating field, with no certainty at all that re-assembly will take place. Sometimes it is a difficult and almost reluctant process and the body is the only resource. The body has to be relied on for its wisdom, memory and, perhaps, will.

Others acknowledge a change of state, sometimes of short duration, sometimes permanent. Others again are aware of little happening in this time and place but very often there is later evidence that a door has opened. There are many doors, perhaps an unlimited number, and the choice to go through them or shut them is ours; although for a few, there is very little choice, only a vocation.

Most change is not at all dramatic. Much of the time, there seem to be constants. Yesterday, Barbara and I were discussing the probability that the house we live in now may well be the last that we share. Not that I won't travel but this is my home, and hers for the last 22 years. It may well be that she stays here too, after I have gone. It belongs to her family and the tenancy is probably secure.

It is Easter and there are family customs around that and the hunting for eggs, painted with one's portrait/caricature, hidden in trees and shrubs in the garden, to be found and boiled for a family breakfast. The number and ages of children, grand-children and great-grand-children, varies, of course, from year to year, but the tradition seems changeless. It is four generations already, which seems great but the timescale is minute in terms of earth-time, never mind the universe.

Three of us live in this house: Barbara, her son, Julian (my stepson) and myself. Many radical changes are taking place for each of us right now, particularly around the subjects of health and occupation – in both cases apparently for the better – which is nice. There is no permanence in either of these fields but we each seem to have some positive outlook right now about these things and about each other.

What we all try to do, of course, is to stop change happening; to resist it. This is the suffering, the resistance. We get old, our friends move, the moths eat the cashmere and the milk goes off. My hair falls out (that was years ago) and my belly sags. I can't stop the changes.

Weird perhaps, to think this way, but it doesn't matter. Night has changed into day, the spring is fantastic, and I have spent half the morning talking with people about the future. That is what is here!

The future, is what I **was** talking about and **is** what I am writing about, right **now**. Past present and future – right here.

Here is a very Zen statement that equates change with time . . . *Life is a journey, not a destination and the only reality is here and now. This moment right now, is no more because this reality goes as soon as it comes, therefore time is an illusion and does not exist!*

I like to say that if we are attentive to the working of the body, on the one hand and the expansions and contractions of the universe and everything in it, on the other hand, we can see the futility of resisting change.

That is what we should not do. Is there anything perhaps that we should do? I would say there is and that is to cultivate a sense of freshness in the moment and its difference to the last moment. This is a continuing and continual expansion of awareness with no finite end. Birth and death, in this paradigm, cease to be absolute events but rather, become signposts, markers, in a continuum of consciousness.

Carl Jung said *We cannot change anything unless we accept it. Condemnation does not liberate, it oppresses.* There is an implication in this that there is a relationship between the illusion of permanence, and judgement. If I think change is a bad thing and that things should remain as they are, or in some views, always were, in the good old days, then I am causing suffering to growth and to myself.

The tide goes out and the tide come is. There is only change.

The tide goes deep and deeper still.
Witness.
I do not hold, it has gone on.
Witness.
Here the pain. Not me to fix.
Witness.
Ever deeper, where now the pain?
Witness.
All doing done, who holds
who is held?
Awareness.
The void
Still in the ocean,
the unformed stirs.
Dark meets light and incarnates.
You and I are we. It was ever thus.
Where now the loss?

Mike Boxhall

12

Intelligence v. Intellect

To do nothing, to just sit in stillness and rely on intelligence itself to restore its affects to equilibrium, is very difficult. Things are noticed and trauma of one kind or another comes into awareness. To then sit and just go deeper into stillness without engaging in the perceived process flies in the face of all our (recent) cultural background. And yet, I believe, this is precisely what we must do in order to work with the Spirit, to get under what is caused to the original causation.

To be attached to what we perceive, to keep our attention on it, is ultimately reductive and will enliven by attention that which we would like to relieve.

What I try to do, with varying success, is to just sit in Stillness and invite the story of another to reveal itself in a space held continually empty. This kind of work is particularly, but not exclusively, effective with babies and children who have yet to build a firmly entrenched life view.

If we think of cause and effect as a sort of family tree, after a few generations the full download will have got very big. If we pay attention to the attributes of one branch of the family, it may lead us back eventually to the original matriarch and patriarch, but we shall have missed out on all the sibling and sub-branches that occurred on the route into the present. So with observing trauma, if we focus on one symptom of what is wrong and try to trace that back to cause, we shall inevitably leave behind a heap of other minor or major branches which devolved from the same route. It is a practice of the body, in its inherent search for homeostasis, to produce another set of symptoms when the first set is inadequately dealt with.

Sitting in stillness, I may notice many different phenomena occurring. It is a fact that I shall not notice all phenomena, but rather those to which my attention is tuned. I can just note these and continue to sit, deepening the stillness through meditation.

My task, then, is not to deal with the symptoms, whatever they may be, but rather to help the patient get in touch with herself at a level which is below that of all symptoms, pain or otherwise, from which level he or she can take a new route back to the surface, unencumbered by the convoluted disempowerments of the past, which have up to now been regarded as the actuality of the present.

I do believe, and it is my experience, that being in physical contact with someone else when one is in a deep level of meditation touches that person at the same deep level, whether it comes into immediate consciousness or not.

The contact is of the order of feather-light, not much more. I am not seeking for anything as such, so there is no resistance from the being of the patient, there is only an outflowing of information at a very deep level, subatomic, for all I know. This information is picked up and recorded at its own level, not that of my intellect, certainly, and is relayed back to the sender, the transmitter. Thus the patient learns who she really is, or at least who she meant to be before layers and layers of life experience clouded that. With awareness comes the possibility for real organic change. This change will be of the being. From that may come change in behaviour – not the same thing. First comes awareness. Without that we are firing bullets into the dark. This is the best I can do with intellectualising what goes on, but I do have hundreds of anecdotal notes to support the observation of Rollin Becker, DO that 'something happened'. I just think I am elaborating a bit more than he chose to do at the time, on what is now the experience of many practitioners.

A short while before writing this I met a new patient, a busy, successful and doubtless highly stressed banker. He had an acute recurrence of a back and neck problem which had been dealt with successfully three years before with a series of half a dozen manipulations. He was in severe pain and suffered restricted mobility in his neck and upper back. I do not do much work with acute back problems; mostly I seem to attract chronic conditions such as depression.

The circumstances of his being booked in were such that he was just there, in a gap due to a cancellation. I started by warning him that my work was, to the observer, a bit like watching paint dry and he seemed to be accepting of the fact that I was not going to manipulate anything. I had been well recommended to him.

I began by taking a comprehensive history, not only of his medical background but also of his domestic and social milieu. I always do this as things may come up in the course of treatment where it is helpful to have a frame of reference to the past, even though we are going to deal with the affects in the present.

I then just sat at his head, having invited him to focus on any sensation arising in the body, whether obviously to do with his problem or not.

For the first few minutes I thought, 'This is a tight skull, nothing much happening here.' I then told myself not to hang around with that thought, just meditate. Gradually I was able to give up the idea of what a problem he was and how I don't/can't do this kind of work, and I noticed that there were the beginnings of some fluctuations. After about ten minutes he said something. I had to ask him what it was, as I was pretty deep into meditation. He said that the pain had spread over to the other side. I think I asked him if he was OK to stay with that, as at least something was moving. He was pretty relaxed and said he was all right with that. After about another fifteen minutes he said in a tone of some surprise, 'It seems to be fading.' I decided that this was not a time to get attached to that idea but to deepen the meditation. After, probably, another twenty minutes, he said very quietly, 'It has gone.'

My summary is that I merely sat in the awareness of meditation with no object, that is to say no attachment to his problem or my own problems, and acted as a fulcrum between his intelligence and mine, at a level which I cannot possibly describe from the intellect.

I hope the pain stays away, as what I think has happened is that he has let go of a negative pattern, a series of life experiences, from the inside. On the previous occasion three years before, the pain was sorted by very skilful manipulation, but this was from the outside. I see this as being the difference and I see this as being empowering to the patient to realise that the release comes from his own re-adaptation, not from being directed. The intellect, while so valuable, remains a limited tool in comparison with intelligence.

To be received in complete stillness empowers the core being of the client to express itself. Rather than the litany of 'this is the story of my undigested life', we get the possibility of the expression of 'this is who I really am at the core of what I express as my conditioning'.

This is a reaction to a piece on stillness from a dear friend and colleague in Spain, Carme Renalias.

> Thanks for the writing. I never have much to say because it just goes in and expands and words leave my mind. All I know is that I am working for many hours giving sessions and it is like a little miracle happening in every session. Intelligence appears!
>
> And sometimes I am just a bit sorry I don't dare to surrender always, all the time, but the experience is there and is the experience that keeps showing me the path, the path to surrender. I am amazed at life when stillness is there, and my heart explodes and tears seem to come to my eyes, with no emotions joined to them, they are just like an expression of love/life/stillness together. And then more surrender and not getting hooked to that, just noticing.

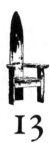

13

Craniosacral Therapy and Meditation

I would like to explain one thing: I have a special affection for a particular type of psychotherapy, called Buddhism. The word 'Buddha' is a Sanskrit word, and it comes from the word *budh*. It means 'awake'. If you wake up, you are a Buddha, how could you not be? Buddha is not a strange, different form of life that you are going to become in 4,000 or 5,000 years, or in 10,000 lifetimes – you are a Buddha right now, just wake up and recognise that. That is all there is. It is not about going somewhere else. There is no other place to go, this is it! You are the Buddha, and you are very beautiful. Wake up a little, please – that's it.

I also have an affection for Craniosacral Therapy and have difficulty in separating my views on that from my understanding of Meditation. This came from a student;

Q: When I am being a therapist, I do nothing, and people often ask me, what is craniosacral therapy? I have to say that I don't really know and that is tough for the clients.

Mike: Yes it is. I agree with you, and a great number of therapists find it extremely difficult to say, 'I don't know.' It is very hard, the intellect doesn't like that. The ego doesn't like that. And then I introduce into this conversation the thought that all knowing is a limitation. Not knowing has infinite possibilities.

You see, it has taken me a long time to arrive at this conclusion. But I really do believe that most therapeutic structurings tend to be also limiting. And that is what I meant when I earlier used the word 'dogma'. I meant that dogma is a limitation. It isn't the model that does the work, it is the relationship between the client and the therapist, or I also call it the synergy, a joint practice, that does the work.

Q: I am practising meditation. Are all meditations valid, or is there some kind of special meditation here?

Mike: No, nothing special. I do not do guided meditation, I do not talk during meditation, I do not play music during meditation. In meditation whatever comes into your mind when you are sitting is your meditation. If you like it, and it is peaceful, that is your meditation. If it is whole load of turbulence like a storm, that is your meditation. If a lot of things happen in your meditation, that is your meditation. If nothing happens in your meditation, then that is your meditation.

Q: So it is a free meditation?

Mike: Sure, it is a free meditation. The fundamental purpose of meditation is to come into the present with what is. Not to get somewhere else. It is the practice of awareness of what is, and then gradually we can remove the judgement of what is. It is quite profound actually; removing judgement is very difficult, because as soon as you remove a judgement, you stop feeding the neurosis that is annoying you with your attention. When you fight your neurosis and try to get rid of it, it like a three-year-old child is getting exactly what it wants, your attention. The nature of the mind is to think, so please do not be a bully to the mind – it is its nature. Stop fighting, leave her to think and gradually . . . ![laughter].

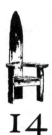

14
Essence and Age

There is a perennial wisdom that pervades all cultures. It manifests time after time after time in different forms according to time, place and space. The form may be dance, speech, painting, poetry, film, sculpture, songs – whatever is indigenous, no one of them can be better than the other, it is quite simply the truth taking form.

The teaching speaks when it is true. It is not the teacher who speaks. She or he is the vehicle of manifestation, not the manifestation.

There is the wisdom of surrender, non-attachment and impermanence: surrender of the tyranny of the habituations I call 'Me'; non-attachment to the past and the future (it is difficult to be attached to the present because it is never stationary); the impermanence of all objects (they are, ultimately, constructs and I am one of them).

The form that I work with is the body. I try to encourage the recovery of the body from its banishment by Descartes to the ignominy of exclusion. The extraordinary thing is that two of the greatest teachers that we have had, Jesus and the Buddha, were both embodied. The Buddha said that enlightenment is in the body and Jesus demonstrated it. I do not teach religion, though, I have an aversion to the dogma which has become attached to it.

Suffering stems from ignorance; the resolution lies in expansion of awareness. Not awareness of data, I would suggest, though data is essential at certain levels, but awareness of what we really are under the undigested life experience with which we identify. It needs composting, incorporating and letting go.

There is nothing new about the search for the truth of Being. It is the mainstay of all heroic journeying through all our histories. It has always been a journey inward, however represented. There is actually no place to go to, only a state of being called awake. It is sensory, as are all the disciplines I listed at the beginning.

I want to justify age a little. I believe that there can be a sensory magic, a great energy released, in the coming together of a small group of people who have lived some life, have a little compost to share, and come together for exchange, conversation, sharing. It is difficult for younger people sometimes to follow the path of the warrior: they want to encumber themselves with armour. The true warrior is possibly the one who takes her armour off. I am leading up to the formation of a (loose) Council of Elders who will meet from time to time and meditate and share experiences.

I remember meeting my first Spiritual teacher, Irina Tweedie. She was a Sufi, Russian by birth, and was lecturing on Hinduism to a largely English audience. I wrote to her out of the blue after the talk, as I knew she was talking to me. It turned out she had a very small group in one tiny room in a rather shabby part of London. I sat with her twice a week for two hours at a time, for two years, in silence. The group grew. By the time she died she sat with 1,500 students very regularly. Teachers do not talk to students, the teaching does. They do help by nourishing themselves, perhaps in the way I have touched on (i.e. by getting together) and by making appropriate conditions available to others.

My vision and my version of my work is something like this.

We all disempower ourselves by hanging on to a sense of who we are, which is actually not who we really are, but a series of life experiences that we carry forward and react from. We are not fully present, we speak, act and even think from what I call our undigested (so not let go of) life experiences.

Someone once told me – made me feel – I was not good enough. This becomes entrenched as a habit, so I never feel good enough. It just is not true, it is a habit!

There are no habits if we are fully in the present. There is only now. What is presence, how do we find it, where is it? The body is present, it always has been. It is the one thing that we can guarantee will be with us as long as we remain alive. I have no desire to get rid of the intellect. It is a superb tool which, arguably, is developing all the time. It is, though, a tool, not who we are. We need to recover somewhat the sensations and feelings of the body in order to live more fully, to love more fully and to become more fully human. We are not just computers.

Finally, the brain is held to be the centre of intellect; the heart is the centre of wisdom. It is a fact that in the embryo the heart starts life on top of the brain and then the body folds to protect the heart. I like that image.

Let us get in touch.

We are shifting mirrors of identity
Aphrodite's playthings; a synthesis of contradictions
Hands and arms link like a golden umbilical cord spiraling
  into the cathedral of my Heart

You play strange notes on my trembling spine as if
re-discovering a long lost cherished piano; a glorious
symphony in Silence

Tumbling child energy awakens forgotten cells and secret
corridors of Remembrance

Held within your chaliced hands,
I pulsate to the red ocean surging under and through me
Sea-stained tears bleed out of this seething molten lava

The sweet scent of Recognition brings serenity and simplicity

I dive into the sea of Grace
Beyond all Tides

And bask in the mystery of Reflection
The astonishing colour of Water
The healing Alchemy of Presence

Jo Féat

Finally, on a light note, this should be sung to the appropriate Gilbert and Sullivan music, at regular intervals, in the presence of all teachers:

When a guru's not engaged in meditation
A-reciting of his mantra for the week,
His capacity for infantile inflation
Is enough to drive disciples up the creek.
He will take the girls aside for tantric yoga
While celibacy is ordered for the chaps;
If he starts behaving like an angry ogre
He will claim it's just to make your pride collapse
Oh, with all this yogic practice to be done,
A disciple's lot is not a happy one.

John Wren Lewis,
(with permission from the estate)

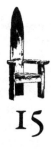

15
Conversations

The Dao is empty – used, but never used up. It is the bottomless source of all things. It blunts sharp edges, unties knots, softens glare, clears dust. It is hidden, but always present. I don't know its mother. It is older than the gods [if there are any gods].

> You need not leave your room.
> Remain sitting at your table and listen.
> You need not even listen, simply wait,
> just learn to become quiet, and still, and solitary.
> The world will freely offer itself to you to be unmasked.
> It has no choice; it will roll in ecstasy at your feet.
>
> (Franz Kafka)

From Gil in Arizona:

Still having different feelings coursing through my body since the class. The most dramatic and important was the intention of using the term Joint Practice when I am working with people. It seems to result in the emptiness that I experienced working with people and yourself.

Do you use the breath in your meditations? It seems to help me to centre and also to invigorate the body. It seems at times to enter the cellular structure and vitalise each cell electrically.

I would be interested to hear what effect your meditative states have on your physicality.

Dear Gil,
I liked what you said about the intentionality to joint practice when working with people. My take on what happens is that this intentionality, so different from 'what can I do for/to you', *itself* puts us in the layer below the trauma, which is usually stuck in the individual or personal or egoic or intellectual – however you want to phrase it. Does this make sense at all? Then, the work does the work as the subject/object differentiations are not there.

If this results in the emptiness, and that is also my experience, then we no longer need the meditation, as the purpose of meditation is to recover (I like that word) the emptiness from which all form arises.

I do use breath in my meditations when, which is quite often, I drift into rambling thoughts or rather start chasing them, rather than watching their coming and going. Breath-watching is then like a route back to focus, which it is, from which I get still enough again that the counting just stops but the state of awareness/presence, attention, remains but with no object, not even the breath.

I don't want to make it sound as if this is easy for me. It is not. What I get much better at is not beating myself up when I fail, just relax about it, honour what is going on, that is awareness, and go back to square one; as if it were no big thing, which it isn't.

If I can do this, I am continually increasing my awareness of what it is to be a human being – not continually judging as though I were outside the process. Maybe this is a description of presence?

It is hard for our culture and particularly our generation to let go of what I call the Protestant work ethic, which is very punishing and judgemental.

I love teaching, as it is then that my practice is a little disciplined. It is not as disciplined as maybe it could be in my day-to-day domestic life. Part of me would love to be a monk but that is not the path I have chosen and I will do my best to incorporate it all. Part of my self-knowledge is that I am not very disciplined about my solo practice. I do know, and people observe, that my practice, not just the meditative states as I do not see them as being something separate, have radically changed my views about crime and punishment – of myself.

I do think that the Cartesian split badly needs healing, but both science and education and to a large extent most spiritual paths are stuck in it. I have to be very careful not to respond to cynics or people who rubbish what I am saying, from that very same place of stuckness.

Dear Mike,
I agree with what you said about going deeper inside of the ego or personality when we use intentionality as in the joint practice and emptiness. I find that to be true in talk therapy with my clients. As the space quiets and the energy in the room changes, which is palpable, then both of us move into a deeper level. Once in that space words seem to spill out of their mouth which seem to be new insights as to how to deal with the problem at hand. This is in direct opposition to the usual invasion of thoughts and analysis by the therapist. I have only been able to come to this in the past year. And that was so great to see it happen in the class with you and others. It is that pure emptiness that is so warming to the soul as it struggles with the bombardment of thoughts and fears.

Yes, the word recover the emptiness is exactly what it feels like when I move into that sacred space. It is like tasting a shaft of light that rested underneath the personality/ego structure. And that is what I felt with you and the lovely group of people we were with.

I too suffer with expectations especially when it comes to the fears that rest in my automatic mind concerning money and whether people will like me. There is an essential fear that drives it and I haven't to this date had a sense of what it is. There were moments in the group that the danger subsided, but it really took flight in my little boy inside and I felt that people didn't approve of what I was saying. As you so eloquently said in your mail, we have to go beyond what the cynics say about the work.

I am so grateful for your words and thoughts. They mirror my own.

Take care of yourself, Mike. Your presence and lack of egoic drive is so refreshing for my soul and Spirit.

Love
Gil

Dear Gil,
I have one more reflection to share with you in this particular correspondence which arises out of your e-mail of the 24th, which is this:

The ego is there and, in my case, anyway, quite often painfully so. It is always there EXCEPT when one is working in a joint practice that is deep enough, that one is coming from, somehow, I don't know how, a level where it *has not yet come into form*! This is true presence.

In the model I propose, we are not trying to somehow get rid of the ego. This would only be to latch further into the Cartesian split and the personal intellect as the tool for the job.

The revelation that can emerge in these conditions comes out of unknowing. A very difficult position for any therapist or teacher to hold. It is, however, as you say, a sacred position/place as it comes from the no beginning, no end, which is the sacred.

I want to try this on you: can we go one stage further than 'Once in that space words seem to spill out of their mouth which seem to be new insights as to how to deal with the problem at hand'? I believe that perhaps we can and that the insights, whether the practitioner's or the client's, are the cure. In themselves, just that! That would be so empowering. Neither party has to DO anything, just BE in the revelation or awareness which IS the new state. The problem can then be seen as being of no inherent substance, just something, a feeling or thought or emotion with which we have temporarily identified.

This would not be to go deeper inside the ego but rather to become the subject of the ego rather than its object. To precede its formation as portrayed in the myth of the revelation of separation, in the Garden of Eden.

This is enormous, of course, and flies in the face of so much didactic teaching, including most models of psychology and all *dogmatic* religion, though not the mystic traditions. Dogmatic religion flirts with absolutes but then *limits the absolute* as being essentially something that is out there. The mystical traditions, most of them, can see no difference between out there and in here, other than realisation.

Some traditions would have us go to war with Maya, Illusion, the Ego and try to destroy it. I would say, in the model of Milarepa, which I love, let us get to know it much better, befriend it, be more fully aware of it as compost until it becomes an important disciple, we could say, expansion. Then, we expand into fuller realisation of our whole identity. Going to war is diminishing. We go to war, not only with the different but we also go to war with awareness. What a pity! The cause is judgement, rather than expansion of awareness.

I find I cannot write great long essays all in one piece as I get distracted and lose the plot, so I will stop here.

Love, Mike

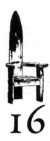

16

Who Does The Work?

In earlier chapters we have discussed topics such as 'let the work, or the synergy, do the work' and have suggested that the more we can get out of the way, the emptier the bowl can be, then the more profound the rebirth into a better adapted, less inhibited form.

The implication has been that the more the personal and restricted ego loosens its hold, the more we shall be in touch with a truer and unlimited self. Work arising from this place that is a communality with all human beings can be very powerful, even life-changing, in the reports of many people.

This is where we run into a little trouble. We have let go of our attachments enough for the work to do the work. Now we fall back into attachment and want to analyse what work has been done and how we can do it again. Surrender and trust are not easy. The uniqueness of each situation, as it reveals, is a readily accepted theory, but what about the maintenance and practice? They have to be continuously worked on, or we are rapidly back where we started, in the personal intellect.

I know so well how easily I want to take credit for some change or improvement. The paradox is that if I were responsible, it wouldn't have happened!

I want to stress this strongly that the further we get out of the way, the greater may be the outcome, but that is because we are out of the way and we have not acquired some power or nostrum with which to heal mankind.

Any moderately successful healer, of whatever persuasion, will have attributes and powers projected onto them. It is important to realise that this projection is from the need of the patient, not a statement of fact. In my view, to take any other view leads eventually and inevitably to aggrandisement and thence abuse.

I have said before that anyone can do this work and I hope that very many more will be encouraged to do so. The only limitation that we all have is our lack of ability to surrender that which keeps us separate from the source – that is to say, our individual life stories with which we have identified so strongly.

The marble or copper or stone or wood statue is not the Buddha. The statue is not the Buddha any more than the Statue of Liberty is freedom. It is a symbol of freedom.

You are the Buddha. Maybe the awareness is a bit clouded, but under all the layers of delusion, that is who you really are.

There is a Tide
I am in the Tide
I am the Tide.

Periodically, argument flares in the media around the existence of God. Eminent people, in their particular fields, speak for one side or the other. The argument is invariably intellectual and while it remains intellectual, people on each side will derive some sense of satisfaction, at an intellectual level, from the force of their argument.

It may be that it does not suit some scientists to visualise the Absolute as Blake's patriarch with long flowing beard and a pair of dividers. I don't know how many people hold to this innocent image.

If, however, as some would hold, there is no mystery and the intellect will, sooner or later, remorselessly explain all, then two things have happened: human intellect has been declared the absolute culmination of evolution, and God has been created by those who deny.

The trouble, in my limited and biased observation, is that Intellect is not always intelligent!

I would rather join Einstein, a scientist of some eminence (though, of course, it is the task of some latter intellects to diminish his achievement in order to stay on top in the pecking order), when he says:

> A human being is part of the whole called by us universe . . . We experience ourselves, our thoughts and feelings as something separate from the rest. A kind of optical delusion of consciousness. This delusion is a kind of prison for us, restricting us to our personal desires and to affection for a few persons nearest to us. Our task must be to free ourselves from the prison by widening our circle of compassion to embrace all living creatures and the whole of nature in its beauty. The true value of a human being is determined by the measure and the sense in which they have obtained liberation from the self. We shall require a substantially new manner of thinking if humanity is to survive.
>
> **Albert Einstein 1954**

Do you know, I rather suspect it will be Intelligence rather than Intellect that helps us survive.

People whose work practice is not different or separate from their meditation or Spiritual practice often ask why, if this way of working produces results, they don't teach it in schools. The answer is quite simple: it cannot be taught in schools. Spirituality is not an object. Schools are often asked what subjects they teach. They do not, of course, teach subjects, they teach objects and this is entirely appropriate. We go to school to acquire information and a structure, building blocks on which we can build an edifice called 'education'. This edifice is essential to our continuation and flourishing as a separate entity that we call 'I'.

That 'I' is capable of great and increasingly complex works in all sorts of fields, as the data and reason of one generation piles on top of the data and reason of the previous generation.

There remain and, I propose, will remain works which self-create outside the supervision of reason – works before which we shall remain in awe, and these are the workings of intelligence itself, an infinite potential of which the intellect is a tiny discrete manifestation.

This is the view of the mystic, quite different from the view of Richard Dawkins and his lack of need for God or a superior and creative Intelligence. Neither of us need worry, however, as levels of being and comprehension are separate.

> In Buddhism, knowledge is regarded as an obstacle to understanding, like a block of ice that stops water from flowing. It is said that if we take one thing to be the truth and cling to it, even if truth comes in person and knocks at our door, we won't open it. For things to reveal themselves to us, we need to be ready to abandon our views about them.
>
> (Thich Nhat Hanh)

Now, that I really like!

17
Doing Nothing

It feels as though I could go on for ever about this subject.

It is so hard in our culture and upbringing to believe that such a thing as doing nothing could be advantageous. We have accepted that we have to be constantly doing and, even more importantly, know what we are doing.

Time after time I invite classes, therapists or not, to work with each other from a place of not knowing. The instructions go something like this:

1. Get the information dialogue, the case history, if you will, out of the way first by listening to the problem as the client presents it.
2. Make sure the client is comfortable on the couch, at least in the physical sense.
3. Sit down beside the couch or mat or chair, whatever you use.
4. Centre yourself. Feel for contact with the ground and the sky. Test yourself to be sure you are present. Am I in touch with my chair, with my feet, with my hands, even with my thinking?
5. Then, and only then, gently make physical contact, wherever seems comfortable to you. If you prefer not to make physical contact, the energetic contact, an intention, is still a contact.
6. Then, *do* nothing! Just receive without commentary, internal or spoken, anything you are offered. Don't judge it; don't analyse it; try not to wonder what it means; just receive what is.

7. Forms, thoughts, patterns, all concepts, will arise. If you engage with them, you have plateaued out and that is where you will stay – which may be very useful, at that level.
8. If, however, you can just stay in the completely open enquiry, other forms will arise, more and more until you reach a level of inter-being where what is there to be declared has been declared. There is a settling, a peace, acknowledged, in my experience, on both sides, that the story has been told. The story has been heard. In the telling and the hearing, there is great healing and the work is done. At least for today.

I think it may be clear that this kind of work does not necessarily demand a therapeutic background. If you can meet the suggestions above, you can do the work. Work with the Spirit is not subject to any intellectual capacity, but rather a complete openness and surrender to what is. That last is the difficult bit, the surrender.

Now let me introduce a spanner into the works: a comment about the reality of doing nothing. It is not possible! Our very presence is a doing. What we can perhaps do, however, is allow the synergy of the relationship to do the work and we just witness that, without intentional engagement with what arises, just with the revelation.

The custom, in our classes, is that after the 'physical contact' session, the group reconvenes in a circle and the experience is discussed, from the point of view of the 'practitioner' and the 'client'. There is clearly, admittedly, a certain artificiality about these relationships, as both parties are at the same time, whichever role they are playing, in a joint and peer practice with each other.

This experience, as it is described, is sometimes apparently similar on both sides. Sometimes it seems to be totally different. I have no difficulty with this, as two people will always have a different experience of any event, simply because they are different people with different sensory mechanisms and different life experiences from which to judge the event. I think I would be quite suspicious, if any group recorded such an event in identical terms, that there were a sort of mass hysteria operating.

What has become clear to many of us, through this process, through this sharing, is the relativity of all experience, that is to say, relative to the time, place, space and the people involved, on the one hand and on the other hand that the most profound life-enhancing experiences have come where the relationship is less of a doing by one to another and more a joint practice between two or more people. I say two or more as, in these circumstances, there are several other pairs in the same room contacting the one energy field. I have no doubt that this magnifies the dynamic.

What is sometimes heard is the following:

M: I felt like he gave me a gift. It was one of those sessions where when I sat down I felt like I could just turn myself loose; for the first time since I'd arrived here. Time was still like the medicine bowl (this refers to a singing bowl that I use to mark the passage of a period of time) yet at the same time there was a different tone to the stillness inside of it. What was beautiful was that everywhere the stillness went and everywhere that my attention was drawn, there were the patterns of his system at that level. It was the first time that there was this crystalline awareness that the patterns are nothing but another faceless form that Jon was wearing.

It just kept unfolding like that. It became every pattern and every thought that might arise in me. Everything that happened in the room was just another face that that stillness was wearing. There was nothing to do but enjoy the ride. When that really started to get big, I was holding his pelvis and suddenly I realised that there was no weight in my hands any more. I thought, 'Oh my god, J. is becoming so light!' I looked at him more directly and the whole pelvic area became this beautiful lotus and every petal was one of those experiences; every petal was one of those patterns of life, but it was all the same stillness.

I think I moved to your [he turns to look at the person he has been talking about] head or shoulders. I don't remember.

There, it was the same thing: just watching and moving through this beautiful, liquid moving stillness and watching these patterns and noting again that it got bigger and bigger. I had to look at my body because I felt like I was just warming my hands by this big fire. The fire was just there; the fire that's in your heart, and the fire that's in the stars, and the fire that is in the centre of our mother [Earth]. It was good.

J: It was a multi-levelled session. I was aware as M. was perceiving these patterns that I could feel the experiences held in my body. 'Oh, that was the time I broke that bone. Oh, that was the time I hurt this.' All of these images of where the patterns came from kept arising in me. Nuances were coming in, and old dreams were coming in, and it felt like wandering through a house, opening a door, and looking in one room after another. I was familiar with every room in the house but I had never recognised that they were all rooms in the same house before. So as M. was perceiving them as petals – I was seeing the lotus as the larger house. In this stillness I was bigger than this injury or this pain, or this pattern, or this reaction; this is more than all of this and it's that as well. It's just another face or part of the house. I don't have any more words for it.

This exchange was part of the report of two practitioners working together, where M. was the client and J. was the therapist. They are both men and experienced practitioners.

The following are feedback notes from a demonstration session by me, where I was at a table with one person, the client, and the rest of the group (about 22 people), the majority of whom were craniosacral therapists, were sitting or lying in the room, with the intention of just receiving whatever dynamic arose in them. They were not focusing on whatever might or might not be going on, on the plinth, table, couch, whatever you want to call it. It was a demonstration of synergy at work in a larger field. I sometimes talk about 'letting the work do the work'. I would say that this can only happen when the practitioner is sufficiently out of the way and not 'doing something' himself, to allow that dynamic of 'the work doing the work' to become apparent. This is some of the feedback from the 'audience'.

N: I was aware of constant change, like moments of being able to be very present. I felt as though I were really embodied and aware of my breath and that felt sense was throughout my whole body. I could also see how the mind was looking to be entertained, so it would often go off into a story or look for something and then I'd drop it and come back to being present. Then the mind would look for another avenue and I would get drowsy and start dozing off. I needed to shift my body to become present again. It was constantly moving through all these different layers.

X: It felt very much like that for me, too and I could hear my attention shifting to the sound of the birds and the sounds from the road, and then I would let go of these and get quiet again. Then something else would attract me and I would think, 'Oh, how easily I am distracted,' and then I'd let go again and just settle. It was a dance. I tried to just be very gentle and not react with, 'Ahh, what am I doing?!'

Mike: Yes that's a much kinder way to work.

A note on presence: it is much misunderstood that presence is not just about being aware of being focused on a target, but equally aware of not being focused on the object one has set out to focus on. If we keep that in mind, we may have less need to beat ourselves up for not being perfect!

Y: I felt a little empty. At one point I felt that I had an awareness of the back of my heart and I felt a gentle oscillation like a motor ticking over. I remembered that I am afraid of motors and I wasn't afraid of this so that was really interesting. I dropped that and then I wanted to lie down, and I thought, 'Oh, I shouldn't lie down,' but anyway, I did.

Mike to A: I think you were going to say something?

A: I got a very physical sensation from the work. I started moving my neck and I could feel something in my heart. When I looked up, I saw this was where your hands were placed [on the 'client']. The main thing I felt throughout was this very deep, sunken feeling in my pelvis.

Mike: Thank you.

Z: I had a really different experience. As I grounded, I felt myself go down into the mother earth and be nurtured and then I sprouted up. I felt like this shoot of me was coming up and I opened up and this seed fell out onto the ground and I thought, 'Well, am I the seed? Just go with it and don't think about it!' I felt this seed open up and the shell or the husk of the seed felt like a bowl [see earlier note on the singing bowl]. My head and my heart felt connected and this seed felt like it was splitting open in between the two. There was so much but that was a really deep experience.

Mike: What a lovely image. Thank you.

Mike to the 'client': How about you, C.? I am interested, because we have not worked before, whether you got in touch with anything at all?

C: I was mostly watching and, similarly to X., I noticed this need to be entertained. I shut my eyes and got some stillness. I actually noticed while it was happening that I was moving my neck in different ways. Then I got real still and I felt my core, and at that point I heard your chair move. I looked and you were moving to the heart area. I took a deep breath and went back in and I started hearing the birds sing, and kind of got lost in something and felt sleepy and then I came back and was present again. In and out, all the time.

Mike: So there definitely was something there for you in the field?

C: Yes, there was.

X: When you first started the session, I was aware that there was a physical bodily reaction to seeing the table go up and the work beginning. I guess it's because it's pretty much what I do all day and my body said, 'OK, here we are, going to work.' It was an interesting awareness. There was a layering of things. I have been juggling a lot and so I was watching all of the thoughts fall and I thought, 'That's OK,' and then like everyone else has said there was this settling into this quiet place. Thoughts would come up and go down. At about the same time, I was able to feel the resonance of when you came up and shifted. Even that sense of the ending was very clear; just this rising up and connecting back. For me it was just an awareness of those current, unconditioned responses.

Mike: Good. What about the fatigue [that she had spoken of earlier]?

X: Oh, the fatigue is just a clear awareness that there are things that I need to or can let go of. Working hard has been, like you said, a life pattern. A kind of circle of having to work hard, and I am still learning to let that go – it is so engrained.

Mike: Any of you guys?

J: I had a scary dream last night and I didn't sleep well. I was just aware of that and trying to be with that this morning. I closed my eyes when the work was going on, on the table and I got this really tender feeling in my chest around my heart. It was so tender I felt like I had to put my hand on my heart just to be with it. When I did that, I felt my heart really expand and I realised that being scared had shrunk this area. It expanded and I feel better now.

Mike: Anybody else?

Y: I am aware not only in this morning's meditation but again now that this is the largest, gender-mixed group that I have been in, doing this kind of work. I have this really wonderful sense of potency of the larger numbers and the horsepower.

Mike: Maybe that's the motor ticking over! [Laughter]

Y: I am finding it very interesting. I am trying to let it be rather than getting into that whole thing of an engine starting up, and thinking, 'Oh, that's a fast car!' I don't have to move fast. I don't have to do anything with it.

Mike: We don't have to look for or expect anything special, anything extraordinary. It may help us though just to get in touch with what is there. Most of the time we don't know what is there. G., do you have any comments?

G: Our connection is so deep that there was no boundary and that boundary-less-ness expanded all the way out, so there were no boundaries between me and anything. The clearest example of that was the singing of the morning dove. The morning dove was no longer out there, it was in here. There was the comfort of being in an empty place.

Mike: I recognise that. There is no separation between two people or twenty-four people. How far can that go? All the people . . . but not only people, of course. In other words, what we call boundaries – separations – are not there. At this level that is useful. At other levels, particularly the mental/emotional level and certainly the physical level, boundaries are very important. Being aware of levels becomes very important. Most psychotherapists talk a lot about boundaries, but I don't quite understand how you can have a boundary against the Spirit. Shock, horror! There are no boundaries [at this level]!

All the comments above represent a certain level of awareness. Other levels of awareness may be there and often are, and they will be reported from time to time in the future. They have equal but different value, as far as I am concerned.

The following comment is from a different course, in another place, at another time, with different people.

L: When P. was working on my head and working on my ears – I felt something loosen in my stomach and go to my head. And that caused a big smile. I had a very strong tension in

> my neck as if someone was trying to strangle me. I asked myself, 'But who is it that wants to strangle me?' And then I realised it was me that wanted to strangle someone else, but instead of doing that I would tense all my body and keep the tension in me. But now this also has loosened. Perhaps just as well! This does seem to be an important awareness, this time at a psycho-emotional level.

I would hazard a guess that most – the vast majority – of the work done by craniosacral therapists is at a psycho-emotional level. Only a small proportion is the purely physical fixing of something and a very small proportion is, either intentionally or not, Spiritual.

The simple reason for this lies in the perceived understanding of what a craniosacral therapist *should* be doing. This, incidentally, probably applies to all job descriptions and therefore, inevitably, to job limitations! Let that description go and you may not know who you are, but you will be able to do unlimited work.

There are many levels of work, of interaction. Perhaps at this point I can just say that all levels are interrelated, co-dependent, co-emergent, however you want to describe it, and the difference is largely a matter of perception. All levels are there all the time. The interesting question is where the awareness is.

Now let's try to summarise. In essence, what we have been discussing doing is, perhaps, the hardest thing there is for any of us to do, which is doing nothing. We have said that, in the literal sense, this is almost impossible.

We have further said that to peacefully watch what we are doing, without getting involved with it, and without judgement, is the next best thing.

If Peace arises out of this work – and that is often reported – then it is a successful session, in my view. I personally know of no more desirable state.

It may be that in that Peace, Intelligence can unravel some of the not-useful habituations that we carry around with us and that we find a better adapted way of Being. I would call that rebirth.

First, the Peace! as any change that comes out of the thinking, rabbiting, attached, judgemental mind will be limited in its scope by the capacity of the intellect and that really is a limitation.

When you stop being a concept, you cease to be something separate and become a Being, not a Doing.

That is what is meant by doing nothing.

18

Teaching

> There is no end. There is no beginning. There is only the passion of life.
>
> **Federico Fellini**

> The practice of mindfulness in these troubled times is more important than ever. If we as individuals do not take the time to practise mindfulness, not only will it be difficult to transform the suffering in our own lives, but it will be difficult to transform the suffering in the world. It is vital to ourselves, our children, and the Earth that we have a practice that helps us to be mindful, that lets us come back to ourselves and dwell in the present moment in order to transform suffering in ourselves and others around us.
>
> **Thich Nhat Hanh**

There is no end to the story; the story is continually being lived and if you are drawn to teach the work, please do so from where you experience it, not where you conceptualise it. That is appropriate for teaching arithmetic, perhaps (though there are mystic mathematicians), but not for Spiritual work.

The teaching is what counts, not the teacher. This is a theme I have consistently promoted throughout my teaching and I think it is worth repeating here.

All my work has been 'leading by following'. As Ray Grigg says in *The Tao of Being*, stanza 30:

> In the Kingdom of thinking, nothing can be obtained by force. Push and thoughts stumble over themselves. Try and there is confusion. Search and struggle and all that is found is searching and struggling. Like moving with the Dao, understanding comes of itself.
>
> The preparation for what comes of itself is called learning. Concentrate on learning and there will be success. Work at understanding and there will be failure.
>
> All learning is learning by following. Learn gently and carefully so the following is not disturbed. Learn with anger and the following leads to fear; learn with fear and the following leads to anger.
>
> To understand, learn and then forget learning. Let go and trust. Understanding comes effortlessly. It is not acquired but happens.
>
> Wonder and soften and open. Let understanding lead. Trust the letting go and follow its leading. This is called understanding-by-following. Let go gently and carefully so the following is not disturbed.
>
> Understanding cannot be controlled by self. Learn to understand by learning to be selfless.
>
> Understanding is thinking free of self, moving uncluttered in the empty fullness of the Dao.

We have tried to follow this dictum and the teaching has been the revelation of what arises when a group of students and a facilitator/teacher are working in joint practice together. This is rather the opposite of a quite common form of teaching which is didactic and dogmatic. I am afraid that this latter does tend to disempower the student, and is rather prevalent.

We would like to see what is there rather than what should be there or what we are told by someone else to expect there to be. It is dangerous to predict the truth. It may turn out that by foretelling it, we reduce it to what we have expected.

The precursor to being able to see what really is, whether in the client or in any other kind of relationship whatsoever, is to be awake. The Buddha not only said that this was his life plan, to be awake; he said, 'I am awake.' There is enormous power in that statement.

So, in the teacher/student grouping, the teacher's job is to be awake to what is present. If the work is not data-based, and ours is not, that may well be all that is required. The work will do the work. No one does something to someone.

Teaching, in this model, is about relationship and what comes out of that relationship, in the presence of right now. That revelation is, necessarily and very uncomfortably, to the intellect, continually changing. There is a continual battle in me between the expression and experience of what arises and the dogma of what should arise or be spoken or be felt.

I am struggling to jump/fall off the cliff into unknowing and trust in what comes out when there is stillness. This will be what I call Intelligence and may have little to do with intellect.

If I can trust that, it will be true and will work. This I experience. If I persuade myself that I am trusting, that is something altogether different and it will not be true and may not work, or at least the work will be very partial and symptomatic.

I do find this very hard sometimes and I do know which level of what I call 'Me' finds it hard.

Practice, practice, practice. That's all there is.

So in the relationship between practitioner and patient, teacher and student, the ever-broadening awareness that unfolds is not an awareness of facts for analysis, but rather an embodying of what is there, deepening by progressive though not necessarily equal steps to a level of being that is untraumatised. I hold this to be experientially true. And I am completely unable to classify or explain what has happened. If I could, I should have objectivised and limited the awakening. To objectivise must, surely, mean to limit. But the work is not an object, any more than is the student/client; there is only a happening, a revelation, movement, change, the nature of all things without separation between the experience and the experiencer.

The beginning and the end are not separate, they are both right here.

That is mindfulness.

This is my method. I hope it has a little wisdom. It is yours.

19

Should I Teach?

People quite often ask me whether I think they are ready or ripe to teach this work, so these are some reflections stemming, largely, from my own experience.

First, let's get the matter of 'levels' out of the way. It seems that every time I try to explain something, I have to say, 'Of course, it depends what level we are talking about.' I think it is probably necessary, however. If we are talking about the most efficient and pain-free way to reset a dislocated little finger, then we have either learned and practised the techniques, or we have not.

If, however, the work we are discussing is of a Spiritual nature and, therefore, in my view, not subject to an objective paradigm of the intellect, then the level and the approach are somewhat different.

In a sense, Spiritual work cannot be taught as though it were an object. What I believe can be done is for the so-called teacher to undertake to create and hold a safe space in which the journey to the light can be undertaken. That is all the teacher can do as the journey is not just that of the 'client/students', but involves the unarmoured surrender of separateness by both/all parties.

It is possible that this laying down of armour-plating, voluntarily, by the teacher is the hardest task that any of us will undertake. It is a labour of Hercules, a voyage of Perseus.

Just when you think you have learned something, acquired a talent, perhaps, let it go.

Who finds it hard? The separate self, the role-attached ego, everything that we have come to think of as being me. That's where the problem is.

I remember well my first attempt at teaching. I gathered together (cajoled/bribed?) a few clients who I considered to be well disposed towards me. I invited a colleague to assist me in case I needed a sounding board. I read and read all the material that I could gather together. I surrounded myself with 20 or 30 books, all tagged with yellow Post-its indicating learned references that I could use to expand my arguments.

The appointed time came and we all sat down and meditated for 40 minutes. The bell rang to indicate the end of meditation and I opened my eyes, looked round the class . . . and had a panic attack. Full blown and remorseless. Only two things stopped me from running out of the room: fear of what people would say or think (see how strong the ego is), and the pile of books!

Arguably, this was the most powerful learning that I have ever experienced. I had to sit and be with the panic attack. I had no option. Something like 40 years later, now that I am in my 80s, I may still not know what I am going to say next until it appears, but I do not care. I just trust, nothing else, and all those 80 years of compost either produce a flower or a weed; it does not matter.

All this is me. Your case is somewhat different. You have already done a considerable amount of work on your own journey to freedom.

The desire to teach sort of wells up like water in a spring and wants to flow out. Consciousness is expanding and teaching has become the latest form that the journey of the Spirit is taking.

You probably just need to wake up – you are actually teaching. Look around at your relationships. What place do you take in your community? How aware are you, compared to how you were, of what is going on? Do people ask you questions (and then insist on giving you the answer, of course)?

Yes, I suspect you are teaching, but you would like to formalise that a little. Then just be clear about that. Take that on board. Digest that this is what you *want*. Great, it is a right livelihood. This action of clarity will have its own effect. You will have energised the 'I want to teach' energy field around yourself and it will come. I do not know what form it will take and I now suggest, 40 years later, in hindsight, that not to construct and limit its form too much will serve you well. What I am doing now – work that I see as an expression of being, rather than something that I do – has little resemblance to the work I thought I was going to do. But that too is an unfolding.

You have nothing to lose, except fear, and you will never get rid of that completely, so you might as well work with it.

Give up expecting results and be amazed at what happens. Jump off the cliff called trust and you may fly. If you don't, try again next time and then really trust, don't just make trust a concept.

When practitioners are drawn towards what may be called Spiritual work, they sometimes get into the false notion that somehow they should not be charging for their work. I offer them this: we chose to be born into human form in a time and space where there is a perfectly valid definition of what right livelihood is. This definition has included, for several hundred years, the idea that money is a means of exchange. That is all. It has no self-worth, it is a means of exchange and not to value, in current terms, what we are offering is to devalue it. It is one of many examples we can find of 'idiot compassion'. To rip people off is to rip people off. To demand a fair wage is just. To support the poor and needy is also just, where that is appropriate.

If you are led to life as a monk and you place yourself at the mercy and generosity of others to support you and you give them healing or wisdom in return, that is fair exchange. So it is if you use cash as that means. Please do not make a judgement about which is better. Something similar arises when people are drawn to teach. 'Am I ready? Do I know enough? Will I get caught out?' All these arise.

These are very valid questions if you want to teach arithmetic or motor mechanics. If you are drawn to something a little different, the only question is, 'Am I prepared to let go of that which keeps me separate from the students? Am I prepared to just be what I am? Can I share that?' Just as it is, without any judgement of good enough or not good enough. The attachment to 'not being good enough' is enormously powerful. It has no substantiality, it is an attachment and the awareness of that opens possibility for change – the change that is at the heart of all phenomena.

If I can share that, the integrity of that will allow the student to realise (to make real or concrete; to give reality or substance to) her own integrity in the joint practice, at all levels, Spirit, Mind and Body.

Notes on teaching: Can I? Should I?

Dear Mike,
I am thinking of starting teaching, some day in the future, even though my own teacher of 'The Teaching not the Teacher' is right here. This day is slowly but firmly coming.

All my life experience, my Buddhist practices, my daily occupation with people, are converging in a natural way to some kind of teaching, similar to yours. Based on emptiness, silence.

I was wondering if you select in some way the participants on your courses. There are many nuances, that, if not taken care of, can cause troubles in the unfolding of workshops. Depending on the nature and needs of the participants.

Do you have something to share on this?

Thanks. See you soon.

Matias

Dear Matias,
I hope you will do this soon.

Dzogchen (a Buddhist form in which we both have an interest and practise) is concerned only with what is. If turbulence is there, then that is what is. I have no guarantees at all about how people will behave. Sometimes a person is there who is having difficulties in being who they are and I have to just work with that.

Usually it turns out to be a blessing but it is sometimes hard to see that immediately.

I am naked. The way of the warrior is to take armour off, not put on more of it. Trust the Tide!

If I selected people in some way I would be dealing only with what I *want*; what is easy for me. This way I deal with what we all *need*.

We can talk more soon.

Love

Mike.

Dear Mike

I love it!

It is very real

And as I feel & see it now,

the only way for me to go.

Of course!!

Thanks.

I have admired your mastery of being naked when facing outbursts from various people.

I need to work on that in me.

Which means,

Shut up.

Open, go on opening!

Matias

I showed Jo this correspondence, as one of my advising team. She responded like this:

Dear Mike,

Thanks for sharing this and I look forward to meeting Matias.

I think you underestimate the skilful means you have in being with conflict and disturbance within individual and group dynamics. Over the years and on many courses with you I have witnessed the courage you have in not veering away from these

> uncomfortable places when they surface, quite often unexpectedly, and with a lot of charge. It can be a huge learning curve for everyone but only if it is held with spaciousness and openness.
>
> This takes quite a lot of hard-earned experience and the willingness to be naked and yet able to respond into the space. Dropping judgement is bloody hard work sometimes!
>
> Lots of love
>
> Jo x

I was grateful, as so often, that I have such people to work with.

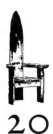

20

Opening or Closing

How to make our lives an embodiment of wisdom and compassion is the greatest challenge spiritual seekers face. The truths we have come to understand need to find their visible expression in our lives. Our every thought, word, or action holds the possibility of being a living expression of clarity and love. It is not enough to be a possessor of wisdom. To believe ourselves to be custodians of truth is to become its opposite, is a direct path to becoming stale, self-righteous, or rigid. Ideas and memories do not hold liberating or healing power.

There is no such state as enlightened retirement, where we can live on the bounty of past attainments. Wisdom is alive only as long as it is lived, understanding is liberating only as long as it is applied. A bulging portfolio of spiritual experiences matters little if it does not have the power to sustain us through the inevitable moments of grief, loss, and change. Knowledge and achievements matter little if we do not yet know how to touch the heart of another and be touched.

(Christina Feldman and Jack Kornfield, 'Stories of the Spirit, Stories of the Heart', from *Everyday Mind*, edited by Jean Smith, a *Tricycle* book)

Years come and go and the memories get longer and the group of those who choose to work together from time to time gets larger.

I cannot doubt that from time to time members of these groups, working in unknowing, as they do, with the revelations that arise in the body, experience some kind of awakening.

Words like profound peace and bliss are often used and there is a sense, visible to all others in the room, that something has profoundly changed. It is mostly evident in the eyes but reinforced by other subtle changes in posture, voice and an awed expression. I believe everyone shares to some extent in the blessing of that expanded presence. It is one person's story, but the whole group has been affected.

Something inside me has reached the place
Where the whole world is within me, breathing.
The flags we cannot see are flying over
The peak of the mountain.
Kabir says: My desire body is dying and my heart's desire is being born.

Kabir

The work is doing the work: that is apparent. It cannot be said that anyone is doing anything *to* anyone; quite simply, creation is happening and we are the witnesses.

Sometimes the person attempts to share with the group the experience of what has been going on. Rarely are the words adequate, in the speaker's perception, to convey the experience. Phrases like chains bursting apart from around the heart are sometimes heard, but often the rebirth is too powerful and tender an experience for there to be words adequate to describe it and we are gifted with the palpable feeling instead of the concept.

This is the euphoric stage, but this is also the stage that we desperately want to hang on to – it is a very seductive attachment, and I liken it to the wet bar of soap in the shower: the harder we grasp, the more elusive it becomes.

We go back to our homes, to the *reality*, the other reality, that we are accustomed and habituated to, outside the safety and support of the retreat centre, and we encounter and are seduced by the old reactive ego patterns which so easily fall back into place. The story is familiar and in its familiarity somehow comfortable, even in its discomfort.

People write to me quite often about how easily they have become bewildered about what it was they brought away from the retreat. What actually did happen, or, indeed, did anything happen, or was it just a dream, a sort of hallucination brought on by the intensity of the group process?

Jack Kornfield sums up this disappointment so well in the title of his excellent book, *After the Ecstacy the Laundry*. Laundry, dishes, mortgages, relationships (perhaps especially relationships), stock markets, wars, the need for a new pair of shoes, the weather – all these things still have to be dealt with. Nothing has changed!

'I need a new teacher. I never did like the way she favoured Charles all the time and I never got a look in.' Perhaps this is a rather childish analogy which doesn't, couldn't, apply to me . . . it sounds like a nine-year-old talking! Yes, it does apply to me, and it does sound like a nine-year-old talking!

And yet, and yet, something has changed. For a moment, back there, we touched the core of being, not just our being but Being, the source of wisdom itself. A faint trace, at least, of that will always be available, waiting to be revisited, rediscovered, where it has always lain, in the heart.

Awareness of what is has expanded not as a concept or intellectual process, but as a felt sense in the body, and that body is there for as long as we shall live.

If the initial coming home to real being, as opposed to disempowered reactivity, is in the body, so then must be the route back to its recovery.

That route is practice. By practice I do not mean sitting for endless hours in a full lotus, or the recitation and repetition of 100,000 mantras, or even the lighting of candles and shaving one's head, although all of these may have value in certain contexts and particularly if not seen as an end in themselves.

The practice I am talking about is being present, time after time for as long as is necessary, to the absolute stark nakedness of what is going on, whether good or bad, and then letting go of both the good and the bad. That is to say, surrendering the judgement.

That is being compassionate, full awareness without judgement. That is what we need and that is the practice for connection with Wisdom, already in place and available all the time.

It was easier in the group, the place where we first had the courage to embark on the way of the warrior and surrender the armour plating. It is easier to be compassionate and supportive to others than to be compassionate towards ourselves, isn't it?

On our own or, possibly, in company with others whose needs are different, it is not easy to allow all the hidden refuse to come to the surface and be accepted as being just what is. The story of a life. Just like that, nothing else. The chances are that if some of it does come to the surface from where we have so laboriously buried it, we shall beat ourselves up with it and add another link to the chain that we haul around.

That is not useful. What is coming up is my life story, nothing more, nothing less. It is there. The only choice I have about it is, having seen what it is, to decide what I am going to do with it. Either I can try to bury it again like some sort of malignant cancer and let it work unseen, or I can compost it. Make it the starting point of right now, the eternal present, not the then that cripples me. All sorts of things can grow from that compost.

The present is the razor blade from which we lick the honey, being vigilant the whole time that we do not cut ourselves on the edge which is complacency and hubris.

There is only practice; there is no knowing the goal as that would be a limitation. It is said that no teacher is free of the possibility of suffering or Mara. Mara lurks and catches us out from time to time and the awareness of that is also the practice. Even enlightenment has its opposite; only change is certain. We keep coming back to the awareness of that and become a relatively still point in an infinite spectrum of change.

What we tasted, in the group, was honey. We can go on collecting honey until the pot is full, and when it is full we must give it away and let others have the taste. Honey is sticky and is easy to become attached to. To obtain the honey, we must surrender that separateness that we have constructed, called 'Me', and become the synergy that we experienced during that time that now seems long ago.

I quite like the idea that we should consciously do what bees do from programming, that is to say, benefit their surroundings while at the same time looking after their own kind.

In our case the locus for our practice is the Wisdom, Intelligence – no confusion with Intellect, which is personal – of the body.

Trungpa Rinpoche said, 'There is no division between the spirituality of the mind and the spirituality of the body; they are both the same.' He commented further that the definition of *samsara* is a mind that parts company with the body. The definition of an awakened person is one for whom there is no separation of mind and body. To know the body is to know awareness. To know awareness in its pure state is to know the awakened state.

The body is present. We cannot walk away from it; we cannot even fly away from it; it is always right where we are and *we know that*, somewhere, somehow, at some level, don't we?

That is where we taste the honey.

> Don't go outside your house to see the flowers –
> My friend, don't bother with that excursion.
> Inside your own body there are flowers . . .
> One has a thousand petals!
> Won't that do for a place to sit?
> Sitting there you will have a glimpse of Reality –
> Inside the body and out, a garden in a garden.
> (Kabir)

People call the experiences I have referred to as Awakenings or Sartori or Kensho – they come in various intensities – and the path to the experience of the next one and perhaps the Great One is letting go the experience of the last one. It could be said that to become attached to any form of experience is to become stagnant right there. Attachment, even to the concept of enlightenment, makes it another link in the chain of disempowerment, and how can that be freedom?

We tend to talk of these openings as doors. There are many doors and an open door may lead anywhere, sometimes, apparently, back to where we started from. And yet it cannot be the same place. Perception has been modified by the travelling of the road. Travel we must, change will be, or the wind of habit will blow the door shut again. That travelling is what we call practice.

We just trust where the road will lead us, we cannot know it in advance without limiting the destination. This trusting we call 'the Blessing of Insecurity'.

The direction of the road is inward towards the heart and this we call 'the Embodiment of Spirit'.

The teacher travels the path together with us and that is joint practice. When, from time to time, the teacher is fully present, we all listen to the teaching not the teacher, which we symbolise by 'the Empty Chair'. 'The Empty Bowl' says it all:

An Empty Bowl

I have a metal bowl.
It was made by the latest in a lineage of such bowl makers.
It is empty, though the Ocean is in it.
If I strike it, it rings and that is useful.
I can put flowers in it, that is beautiful and that is useful but it won't ring.
My grandson could pee in it and probably would and that would be useful but it would not ring.
If I approach it from stillness and get into joint practice with it, it sings beautifully
And the sound goes all round the universe
And that is very useful
And the bowl is empty.

I have a mind.
It was made in eternity.

And if thoughts are in it, that is useful.
And if lesions are in it and edges of resistance, that is useful.
And sometimes it is full of roses and sometimes full of piss
  and I can work with that and that is useful.
But if it is empty and I can approach another in stillness,
There is room for the whole story and she remembers who she
  really is and the universe remembers what it is
and that is really useful.
And the mind is empty.

(Mike Boxhall)

The flowers bloom. The flowers die. The seeds fall. The end is the beginning.

Let us welcome today.

About the Author

'You are old, father William, the young man said,
and your hair has turned very white,
and yet, you continually stand on your head.
Do you think, at your age, it is right?'

**Lewis Carroll in Alice's
Adventures in Wonderland (1865)**

Well, that just about sums it up!

On a recent North Carolina course, I was grilled by the students for a biography. Nearing 80, I had forgotten most of it, but judicious questions from my wife, who bravely attended the course, mostly starting 'Yes but, what about when . . .' got some of it out of me. At least, the bits I was *prepared* to remember.

I am married to Barbara and, in true British understatement, this is a good thing! I was married before and each of those ventures seemed like a good thing at the time. This one gets better. The others got worse. Be an optimist, anyone who is not sure; kiss a few toads!

We have four children, three of mine and one of hers. There were eleven grandchildren the last time I counted, including grand-nephews/nieces.

We live in a tiny cottage in the south of England and have a lovely garden, a passion of both of us. I grow organic vegetables and she grows flowers.

Career-wise, it appears from records that I have been a clerk (for my dad), a rubber-planter in Malaya, a soldier in the jungle, an international film distribution executive (great expense account), a dealer in Bruce Lee pictures, an organic food store manager, a counsellor, a psychotherapist, an acupuncturist, a craniosacral therapist . . . and whatever the future will bring.

I have been a therapist for about 40 years.

I have been a Buddhist for about 40 years.

All the above, and some other facts that I won't bother you with, is called 'compost'. Oh, and I used to be an athlete, but that was a really long time ago. Now I feel very mortal.

It all comes together in what I try to teach, which is, in the meaning of words of the Buddha, that enlightenment is in the body. Right here and right now.

The felt sense of this started emerging when I trained in craniosacral therapy with Franklyn Sills in his early teaching days before the Karuna Institute was formed. I much valued that teaching – and still do. It has led me to evolve my own style, just as he evolved his, out of his previous work. I wish everyone would teach their own story rather than recycle someone else's with the inevitable consequent loss of integrity.

I hope that this book has demonstrated that the essence of what I now see the work as being is surrender. We could say that what has been required has been the surrender of Intellect to Intelligence. It is a good deal: new lamps for old, or, in this case, the limited constructs of the personal for the infinite potential of the communality.

This is the path. This is the road that hopefully we shall each continue practising. Practice is important. The personal, separated self does not easily give up the struggle to remain top dog, in fact the only dog in town. Joint practice, unity, is not the ego's natural playground.

Further background

I teach a series of courses over a number of modules, which gradually step down to working totally in the present from the Stillness of the unknown, i.e. that which has not yet come into form, the form that defines and limits. Currently I do this on a regular basis in the US, the UK, Italy, Spain and Ireland.

I deeply love my family, my work, my students, my surroundings, and I tend to be workaholic. I have instructions from higher authority about that and must slow down. This means that I shall, in the long term, make less and less long-haul flights, which I find exhausting, and will focus on teaching where people largely come to me, or I go to some nice place in Europe. I suspect that the ink will not be dry on that last statement before I shall be asked to do something in Tokyo!

Clinically, I went from reasonable success in working with infertility in women to working with babies, where I am slightly controversial in some quarters as I trust their intelligence, not my intellect. I learned the stuff I teach adults from working with babies, not the other way round.

I have addressed the Breath of Life Conferences in the UK and the US on several occasions as keynote speaker and gave a keynote talk in Spain last year on the occasion of the Association's tenth anniversary. I am a member of various teaching faculties.

Over the last several years the teaching has evolved, out of input from students, away from the benignly mechanical to the completely revelationary.

There is, with your future help, much more to explore in this quest to expand awareness – awareness not only of the nature of who we really are, but further, the health that is the ground of that nature.

Teachers

Among those from whom I have learned and continue to learn so much are, chronologically:

Milarepa, tearaway and then saint
Carl Gustav Jung, visionary
Joe Redfern, psychoanalyst and Jungian training analyst

Professor Jack Worsley, who understood the meaning of presence and intuition, acupuncturist
Irina Tweedie, a Sufi who walked her talk, at whose feet I was happy to sit twice a week for two hours for two years
Chogyam Trungpa, tearaway and saint in parallel, Dzogchen Buddhist
Ian Gordon Brown, who put me in touch with reality, transpersonal psychology teacher
Franklyn Sills, who put me in touch with levels in the body, craniosacral teacher
James Low, psychotherapist, Buddhist scholar, supervisor and friend
My students
My family
Barbara

I am all of these and none of these. I stand on their shoulders in gratitude.

People know me as a therapist. I recognise that label and that is what I do. It may not be who I am, but that is another story. For half of my 80 years I have been a practising therapist: a counsellor, an acupuncturist and, for many years now, a craniosacral therapist. For the last 15 years, or so I have been teaching. In the course of teaching, I have come to realise that, whatever we do, whether it is a therapy or not, what needs real attention is where we are coming from when we do what we do. I give this precedence over the techniques of the form of what we are doing. This is certainly not the intellectual or scientific approach; it demands continuing awareness, in stillness, to what is revealing itself right now, without diagnosis, prognosis or remedy.

This could seem to be anarchic and it is not easy. It is a state of unknowing in which there are no answers, only revelation. The final expression of revelation is the core, or heart, where there is no pathology. Description of any kind must always remain a poor substitute for experience; the experience is available to us all.

Book List

The following is a list of books that have been influential, not only in the writing of this book directly, but also on my life in general, out of which experience this book has emerged. The list is not exhaustive but is a fair representation of my working library. The order is alphabetical by author's surname.

Adyashanti, *Emptiness Dancing,* Sounds True, Boulder, 2004

Armstrong, Karen, *The Case for God*, Bodley Head, London, 2007

Balsekar, Ramesh, *Advaita on Zen and Tao,* Yogi Impression Books Pvt, Ltd. Mumbai, 2008

Balsekar, Ramesh, *Who Cares?!* Zen Publications, Mumbai, 1999

Barnhart, Bruno, *The Future of Wisdom,* Continuum International Publishing Group, New York, 2007

Barrow, John D., *The Book of Nothing,* Vintage, London, 2000

Batchelor, Stephen, *Buddhism Without Beliefs,* Riverhead Books, New York, 1998

Batchelor, Stephen, *Verses from the Center*, Riverhead Books, New York, 2000

Batchelor, Stephen, *Confession of a Buddhist Atheist*, Spiegel & Grau, New York, 2010

Boyce, Barry (Editor), *In the Face of Fear*, Shambala, Boston, 2009

Brazier, Caroline, *Buddhist Psychology*, Robinson, London, 2003

Capra, Fritjof, *The Tao of Physics,* Shambala, Boston, 1975

Capra, Fritjof, *The Turning Point*, Simon and Shuster, New York, 1982

Capra, Fritjof, *The Web of Life*, Harper Collins, London, 1996.
Carrol, Lewis, *Alice's Adventures in Wonderland and Through the Looking Glass,* Penguin Classics, London, 2003
Carse, David, *Brilliant Perfect Stillness,* Paragate Publishing, Shelburne, 2006
Chang, Garma C.C., *The Hundred Thousand Songs of Malarepa,* Shambala, Boston, 1989
Chopra, Deepak, *Quantum Healing,* Bantam Books, New York, 1989
Chopra, Deepak, *How to Know God*, Rider, London, 2000.
Coelho, Paulo, *The Alchemist*, Harper Collins, London, 1993
Coelho, Paulo, *Manual of the Warrior of Light*, Harper Collins, London, 2002
Damasio, Antonio R, *The Feeling of What Happens,* First Harvest, Orlando, 2000
Das, Lama Surya, *Awakening the Buddha Within*, Bantam Books, London, 2007
Dowman, Keith, *Natural Perfection,* Wisdom, Boston, 2010
Epstein, Mark, M.D., *Thoughts Without a Thinker*, Basic Books, New York, 1995
Epstein, Mark, M.D., *Going to Pieces Without Falling Apart*, Broadway Boos, New York, 1999
Epstein, Mark, M.D., *Going on Being,* Wisdom Publications, Somerville MA, 2001
Foster, Jeff, *Life Without a Centre,* Non-Duality Press, Salisbury, 2006
Foster, Jeff, *Beyond Awakening,* Non-Duality Press, Salisbury, 2007
Fromm, Eric, *To Have or to Be,* Jonathan Cape, London, 1978
Goleman, Daniel with the Dalai Lama, *Destructive Emotions*, Bloomsbury, London, 2003
Greene, Brian, *The Elegant Universe*, Vintage, London, 2000
Greene, Brian, *The Fabric of the Cosmos,* Penguin Books, London, 2000
Gribbin, John, *In Search of Schrödinger's Cat*, Wildwood House, 1984
Gribbin, John, *Schrödinger's Kittens,* Phoenix, London, 1996
Grigg, Ray, *The Tao of Being,* Wildwood House, Aldershot, 1989
Hanh, Thich Nhat, *Being Peace,* Parallax Press, Berkeley, Cal, 1987

Hanh, Thich Nhat, *The Heart of the Buddha's Teaching*, Parallax Press, Berkeley, Cal, 1998
Hanh, Thich Nhat, *Living Buddha, Living Christ,* Beacon Press, Boston, 1999
Hanh, Thich Nhat, *No Death, No Fear*, Riverhead, New York, 2002
Hawking, Stephen, *A Brief History of Time,* Bantam, London, 1998
Hayman, Ronald, *Nietzsche*, Phoenix, London, 1997
Heider, John, *The Tao of Leadership*. Wildwood House, Aldershot, 1986
Hellinger, Bert, *Acknowledging What Is,* Zeig, Tucker and Co, Phoenix, 1999
Hofstadter, Douglas, *I am a Strange Loop,* Basic Books, New York, 2007
Kenton, Leslie, *Passage to Power,* Vermillion, London, 1996
Khema, Ayya, *Being Nobody, Going Nowhere,* Wisdom Publications, Boston, Mass, 1987
Khyentse, Dzongsar Jamyang, *What Makes You Not a Buddhist,* Shambala, Boston, 2007
Kohn, Azima Melita and Mafi, Maryam, (Translators) *Rumi, Hidden Music*, Thorsons, London, 2001
Kornfield, Jack, *A Path With Heart,* Bantam Books, London, 1993
Kornfield, Jack, *After The Ecstasy, the Laundry,* Bantam Books, London, 2000
Krishnamurti and Bohm, David, *The Ending of Time,* Victor Gollanz 1985
Lao Tzu, (Richard Wilhelm edition) *Tao Te Ching*, Arkana, London, 1985
Laszlo, Ervin, *The Whispering Pond,* Element Books, Rockport, 1996.
Lovelock, James, *The Ages of Gaia,* Oxford University Press, Oxford, 1989
Low, James, *Simply Being,* Vajra Press, London, 1994
McGilchrist, Ian, *The Master and His Emissary,* Yale University Press, Newhaven, 2009
McTaggart, Lynne, *The Field*, Harper Collins, London, 2001
Mello, Anthony de, *The Heart of the Enlightened*, Doubleday, New York, 1989

Needleman, Jacob, *Lost Christianity,* Jeremy K. Tarcher/Penguin. New York, 2003
Needleman, Jacob, *The Wisdom of Love,* Morning Light Press, Sandpoint, 2005
Needleman, Jacob, *What is GOD?* Jeremy K. Tarcher/Penguin, New York, 2009
Nepo, Mark, *Surviving Has Made Me Crazy,* Kavan Kerry Press, New Jersey, 2007
Nepo, Mark, *Facing the Lion, Being the Lion*, Conari Press, San Francisco CA, 2007
Nepo, Mark, *The Book of Awakening*, Conari Press, San Francisco CA, 2011
Nichol, Lee, (Editor) *The Essential David Bohm,* Routledge, London, 2003
Norbu, Namkhai, *Dzogchen, the Self-Perfected State,* The Penguin Group, London, 1989
Packer, Toni, *The Light of Discovery*, Shambala, Boston, 1995
Parsons, Tony, *The Open Secret,* The Connections, Cornwall, 1995
Pierce Brian J., *We Walk the Path Together,* Orbis Books, New York, 2005
Ralpula, Walpola, *What the Buddha Taught,* Atlantic Books, New York, 1974
Ridley, Matt, *Genome*, Fourth Estate, London, 1999
Ringu, Tulku, *The Lazy Lama Looks at the Four Noble Truths,* Bodicharia Publications, Scotland, 1999
Roy, Arundhati, *The God of Small Things,* Random House, New York 1997
Satre, Jean-Paul, *Being and Nothingness*, Citadel Press, New York, 1956
Sheldrake, Rupert, *A New Science of Life*, Flamingo, London, 1995
Sheldrake, Rupert, *The Presence of the Past*, Park Street Press, Rochester, 1995
Sills, Franklyn, *Craniosacral Biodynamics,* North Atlantic Books, Berkeley, California, 1947
Smullyan, Raymond M, *The Tao is Silent*, Harper, San Francisco, 1992

Sogyal, Rimpoche, *The Tibetan Book of Living and Dying*, Rider, London, 1992
Suchito, Venerable Ajahn, *The Path to the Deathless*, Amaravati Publications, Hemel Hempstead, 1987
Suzuki, Shunryu, *Zen Mind, Beginners Mind,* Weatherhill, New York, 1970
Swimme, Brian, *The Hidden Heart of the Cosmos,* Orbis Books, New York, 1996
Thurman, Robert A.F., (translator) *The Tibetan Book of the Dead,* Thorsons, London, 1995
Tolle, Eckhart, *The Power of Now*, Hodder and Stoughton, London, 2001
Trungpa, Chogyam, *Cutting Trough Spiritual Materialism*, Watkins, London, 1978
Trungpa, Chogyam, *The Myth of Freedom,* Shambala, Boston, 1988
Trungpa, Chogyam, *Crazy Wisdom,* Shambala, Boston, 1991
Tweedie, Irina, *The Chasm of Fire*, Harper Collins, London, 1979
Walsch, Neale Donald, *How to Know God,* Hodder and Stoughton, London, 1995
Watts, Alan, *The Wisdom of Insecurity,* Rider, London, 1992
Watts, Alan, *Tao, the Watercourse Way,* Arkana, London, 1992
Wegela, Karel Kissel, *How to Be a Help Instead of a Nuisance,* Shambala, Boston, 1996
Wilbur, Ken (editor), *The Holographic Paradigm Shambala, Boston, 1985*
Wilbur, Ken, *The Eye of Spirit*, Shambala, Boston, 1998
Wilbur, Ken, *One Taste*, Shambala, Boston, 2000
Zinn, Jon Kabat, *Wherever You Go, There You Are,* Hyperion Books, New York, 1994
Zohar, Danah and Marshall, Ian, *Spiritual Intelligence, the Ultimate Intelligence*, Bloomsbury, London, 2000
Zukav, Gary, *The Dancing Wu Li Masters,* Rider, London, 1979

Index